# The
# Common
# Denominator

*Clara Petty*

authorHOUSE®

*AuthorHouse*™
*1663 Liberty Drive*
*Bloomington, IN 47403*
*www.authorhouse.com*
*Phone: 1 (800) 839-8640*

*Published by AuthorHouse  03/08/2017*

*Library of Congress Control Number: 2017903159*

*ISBN: 978-1-5246-7427-4 (sc)*
*ISBN: 978-1-5246-7426-7 (e)*

# Contents

*For my sons and grandchildren…*
*Of all I have done in my life, I am most proud to be your*
*Mother and Grandmother*

# Acknowledgments

My thanks to the many friends, family, and professionals who helped make this book possible. Especially to David Cisel, whose input on teen pregnancy was invaluable. Many thanks to friends Alene Darnell, Lou French, and Ellen Riker, and to the Memphis *Commercial Appeal* for their contribution.

# Preface

A Hero is an ordinary individual who
finds the strength to persevere and endure
in spite of overwhelming obstacles.

—Christopher Reeve

My passion is people. I have a passion for helping people
reach their goals and dreams. To know that I have touched
a life, or have helped people or inspired them in some way
is invaluable. Coming from poverty, I have a huge heart
for the underprivileged. My mission is to help break the
cycle of despair long before the doors are slammed shut.

In an effort to plant seeds of hope and encouragement,
my desire is that this book be an example of learning to
believe in oneself and in the importance of never giving up.

As I found with my first publication, *The Sharecropper's
Daughter*, writing a book is a very personal and sometimes
gut-wrenching experience. I expect criticism from both
the far right and the far left regarding *The Common
Denominator*. I realize criticism is inevitable from those on
both sides who "may or may not agree from their points
of view." But, as with my first book, I am determined to

write what I believe is honest and right. Growing up in the Deep South, I know racism at its worst. The contents of this book are in no way intended to be racist, but are facts intended to inspire us all to use our God-given talents to improve our lives, our communities, and our country. I realize this is a subject of considerable controversy, but this city and our country simply must not ignore it any longer. If we do not face the problem, it will never be fixed.

After the success of the civil rights movement, both political parties enacted federal and state programs to take care of the indigent. With all good intentions, both Republican and Democratic politicians removed much of the pride of accomplishment that comes from hard work and self-reliance as millions found that dependence on the government was preferable to hard work and self-reliance.

Unfortunately, our leaders failed to realize the long-term negative effects that would result from taking away the incentive to be self-supporting and the value of personal responsibility versus governmental responsibility.

It is my hope that this book will shine a light on policies and procedures currently in place that were intended to aid those who cannot help themselves and that we, as a country and a people, can work together to come to a more workable solution.

· · · · · · ●●● ●●● · · · · · · ·

From the days of separate schools, separate water fountains, and separate eating establishments, tremendous strides have been made by our African American population in the last fifty years.

Although slavery had long been abolished, racism was still rampant in the 1960s when civil rights became a rallying cry. Black achievement since the civil rights movement is a source of pride. We had the first black president in the nation's history. The number of blacks with college degrees is three times what it was in 1970.

African Americans have made numerous significant contributions to the welfare of our country. Although Thomas Edison is credited with inventing the light bulb, it was his black assistant, Louis Latimer, who invented the filament for the light bulb. Latimer also invented the electric lamp and played an important role in assisting Alexander Graham Bell with invention of the telephone. Barrett Morgan, an African American, invented the traffic signal and gas mask.

Many of the modern conveniences we now take for granted were invented by African Americans who were once slaves.

Carl Rowan, a young black man from Tennessee who grew up in a shack with no electricity, no heat, no running water, no toilet, and never enough food, clawed his way through poverty and racism to become one of the first black naval officers in World War II and one of the first blacks to work on a major newspaper, the *Minneapolis Tribune*. He was appointed by President Kennedy to serve as ambassador to Finland and later served under President Johnson as head of the US Information Agency. Rowan is the author of the bestselling book *Breaking Barriers*.

More recently, African American Dr. Ben Carson's personal ascent from inner-city poverty to an internationally renowned neurosurgeon and humanitarian is a role model for all—regardless of race, creed, religion, and socioeconomic status. Dr. Carson is professor of neurosurgery, plastic surgery, oncology, and pediatrics, and the director of Pediatric Neurosurgery at John Hopkins Medical Center. He is a recipient of the Presidential Medal of Freedom, the highest civil honor in America

Dr. Carson, an amazing man and a giving person who is always looking for ways to make life better for others, is also the author of four bestselling books. In his book *America the Beautiful*, Dr. Carson gives a real-life prescription that could cause our great country to again reclaim the values that made her great in the first place.

Included among my favorite authors are African Americans Maya Angelou and Star Parker. The late Maya Angelou is the author of seven autobiographies, including one of my favorites: *I Know Why the Caged Bird Sings*. Among her many famous quotes is one that resonates in today's world: "Looking around at our world it is time to rebuild new bridges and reach each other with a love that can no longer be ignored or abandoned."

Star Parker, appropriately named as she is a true star, rose from the ranks of poverty and the welfare system to become a syndicated columnist as well as a regular commentator on CNN, CNBC, CBN, Fox News, and the United Kingdom. She is founder and president of CURE (the Center for Urban Renewal and Education), a 501-nonprofit think tank that provides a national voice of reason on issues of race and poverty in the media and inner-city neighborhoods.

· · · · · · · ● · · · · · · · · ·

For more than four hundred years, my Native American ancestors were deceived, corralled, forced onto small pieces of land, and discriminated against. They were called dirty Indians, Injuns, redskins, and savages. They couldn't get jobs or buy homes. October 2016 marked the 178th anniversary of the Trail of Tears when the Cherokee Indians were removed from their homes in Georgia, Alabama, and Tennessee as part of the government's Indian Removal Act of 1830. Some twelve thousand men, women, and children in ragged clothes, many of them with only cloth to wrap their feet and blankets for coats, were forced to walk nine hundred miles to their new homes in the "Indian territory." Along the way, thousands died of starvation, illness, and exposure.

What happened to the Indians wasn't a fair fight. Their land was stolen, their religion was forbidden, and they were forced to bend to foreign domination. As with slavery and the early treatment of African Americans, what happened to the American Indians wasn't okay.

· · · · · · · ● · · · · · · · · ·

Today's real-life heroes are those who have become successful despite past struggles and deep wounds. These amazing heroes developed an early understanding that prosperity does not come from government dependency, but from men and women who value honesty, integrity, character, and morals, and who are achieving the American dream through self-reliance, hard work, faith, family, and responsibility.

These heroes found their way because of who they are. They sowed their own seeds of hope. They chose what to make of their lives, reaching their highest potential by nourishing that hope into reality.

# Introduction

> No matter how big your house is, how recent
> your car is, how big your bank account; our
> graves will be the same size—Stay Humble.
> —Unknown

To say times were tough does not begin to describe my life growing up. My parents were good, hard-working people who struggled mightily to put food on the table for our seven-member family. Eking out an existence on a small farm in eastern Arkansas, we grew our own food and worked hard to make ends meet. We worked that rural plot as if our lives depended on it because, in all probability, it did.

Despite growing up with no indoor bathroom, no running water, no TV or telephone, and no air conditioning, my four siblings and I grew into successful, productive adults. We are proud to be living examples that personal success is not about government programs, but about taking personal responsibility. That freedom is about doing the best you can for yourself and others, not about being enslaved to the government.

I fell in love with reading at an early age. We were very poor, but between the pages of books, I could go anywhere, I could be anybody, and I could do anything. I hated being poor, and reading afforded an escape from our everyday poverty and sense of hopelessness.

I loved reading about people of great accomplishments. As I read their stories, I began to see a connecting thread. I began to see that the person who had the most to do with me and what happened to me in life was me. I could choose my destiny with determined personal effort. I didn't have to depend on what someone else did or what someone else gave me in order to be successful. I had to make decisions, and I had to decide how much energy I wanted to put behind those decisions.

Growing up, I was, and still am, a very determined person. I always thought I was in charge of my own destiny. Craving opportunity, I felt education was the key. However, obtaining even a high school education was a Herculean task. It took extra doses of motivation, discipline, courage, determination, persistence, and a lot of tears.

According to the odds I was born into, my life was not supposed to be one of academic achievement, much less a writer. I didn't write this book because I've accomplished anything extraordinary. I wrote this book because I've achieved something quite ordinary, which in all probability doesn't happen to most people who grew up like me. But determination kicked in as I reminded myself, "It's not where you come from or where you lived, it's the choices you make in life."

I was one of five children born into the Adkins family. In my early years, my father was a sharecropper and then a tenant farmer. We were a poor family that grew cotton for a living in the Arkansas Delta. Producing a cotton crop is labor intensive, working long hours in the intense southern heat. My siblings and I were expected to work like adults to help support the family. There was rarely time to play or even go to school until the annual cotton crop was harvested.

In the early 1940s we lived in a four-room house with no electricity, no running water, and no indoor bathroom. A few years later we moved into a house on Crowley's Ridge in the New Castle community near the small town of Forrest City, Arkansas. Since the house was larger and had electricity, it was an improvement over the previous one. Still, with no indoor bathroom, daily visits to the outhouse in the cold of winter encouraged us to make our visits as short as possible.

Life was very different in those days. Most of the "things" we have today, we did not have back then. Our lights were kerosene lamps. Our central air was the cardboard fans that had been donated to the church by the local funeral home. Our central heat was the wood-burning stove we used during the winter with wood brought in each night. There were no supermarkets. Sunday dinner usually consisted of fried chicken that came from the backyard chickens Mama killed, plucked, and cooked. If we didn't eat what Mama cooked, we didn't eat.

Milk came from a cow we milked the night before; butter was churned from the same milk. When the kitchen was cleaned and dishes washed after meals, our sink was a pan on the kitchen table filled with water and another next to it filled with water for rinsing. The running water was when we drew it from a cistern. We bathed in the same tubs we used to do laundry. We did not have carpet, just wood floors covered with cheap linoleum. We did not have television or a telephone until my high school days.

We all learned hard work early. Time was something we did not waste, and we didn't put off until tomorrow what we could do that day. A wake-up call was when Mama called out, "It's time to get up!" and she meant right then. Daylight-saving time was when we were in the field at 6:00 a.m. and got home at 6:00 p.m. A wristwatch was when Mama summoned Daddy from the field by beating on an iron plate with a hammer. The only timepiece was the white alarm clock that was dutifully wound as the last sound heard before falling asleep at night.

Texting was when Mama called from the back porch saying, "It's time to come in!" E-mail was the letter we mailed for three cents. Video games for us were hopscotch, jump rope, and jacks. The mouse was what we set a trap for in the kitchen. Pot was what Mama used to cook beans and turnip greens.

Long distance was when we walked to the house after a long, hard day in the fields. The fast lane was the gravel road we took to Horton's country store, or to a relative's or neighbor's house. Rap was when we knocked on the door of a neighbor's house to borrow a cup of sugar. Gun control was how steady you held your rifle.

The weatherman was when Mama or Daddy looked outside and said, "It looks like a cloud is coming up." The temperature was cold, warm, hot, or very hot. We didn't use numbers such as thirty, sixty, or eighty degrees when we discussed the weather. Discipline was when we heard, "No," and got that "look" from Daddy. Nothing else was necessary.

Growing up, our curfew was the lightning bugs we liked to catch in Mason jars and stick on our fingernails to watch them light up. Our parents didn't call our cells; they yelled our names. We played outside, not online or on an Xbox. "Online" meant the clothes that were hung on a clothesline to dry: summertime, wintertime—every Monday.

Wallpaper, often considered a luxury today, served a dual purpose for our family. Not only did it cover the ugly walls, but during winter months it prevented the cold air from coming through the cracks and crevices. Since wallpaper paste was considered too expensive to buy, Mama used a mixture of flour and water to make her own. While not having the sticking power of a commercial product, it was more affordable.

We did a lot of repairing, especially during cold weather, when the wood heater would dry the flour paste, causing the wallpaper to crack and loosen. You could hear the snap, crackle, and pop all through the night. The next day you may see dangling pieces of wallpaper or a bulge where the paper came loose from the wall and created a giant bubble.

We usually had at least one cow, which provided daily products for the family: milk, butter, and buttermilk. The taste of fresh milk straight from the cow was very different from pasteurized milk. One of our most dreaded chores was milking the cow. Daddy usually did this, but sometimes when darkness was approaching, and he would still be in the field, the job would fall to Mama or one of us kids.

Of the myriad problems associated with milking a cow, one was the cow's sensing your nervousness and refusing to "let her milk down." The constant swishing of her tail back and forth slapped you in the face with each motion.

One Saturday afternoon after washing and rolling my hair in pin curls using bobby pins, I was sent to the barn to milk the cow. It was late summer, and the cows had been grazing in the back pasture, which was filled with dried cockleburs. As I sat on the milking stool to begin milking, that cocklebur-filled tail began swishing, catching on my pin curls and hanging on the bobby pins. My screaming startled the cow, and she began running with me hanging onto her tail for dear life as Mama, hearing my screams, came to my rescue.

· · · · · · · ● ● ● ● ● ● ● · · · · · ·

Being from a generation where it was usual for children to join in the cotton harvest, my father did not let attending school get in the way of getting the cotton crop in during fall harvest. From nine years of age through high school, I attended school only seven months of the year, missing the important beginning of school during September and October. It was an awkward battle fought silently, as we never questioned Daddy's decisions.

One of my most poignant childhood memories was watching with envy as I looked up from my cotton row and through tears, watched the yellow school bus loaded with children pass down the gravel road. There are few things in life I wanted as badly as I wanted to be on that school bus. I thought kids who got to go to school all year were the luckiest people on earth.

After the cotton crop was harvested, I was allowed to start school, usually around the first of November. Already two months behind the other students, entering school late was traumatic, fostering feelings of insecurity and wondering what others thought as I entered each class and had to meet with the teacher to be assigned a seat.

Driven by the knowledge that there was something better than the cotton field and a determination to make a better life, I took education very seriously. Cramming a whole school term into seven months did not keep me from striving to be one of the best. At the start of each school year—although two months behind the other students—I would somehow manage to catch up and excel, even earning an academic college scholarship my junior year.

During my high school days, it seemed I was always trying to get somewhere better while the rest of the school rushed by not noticing me trudging along in their midst.

I was not one of the more popular students; I was not a cheerleader; I was never president of anything, but that was okay because I was planning my future, and that future had nothing to do with the cotton patch.

As a child growing up in a poor environment, I loved to go to school. My passion for learning would sometimes attract a teacher's attention, and I would become the "teacher's pet." I idolized my teachers, and words of encouragement from some of them greatly influenced my life and the person I became. I can vividly remember the words of one of my favorite teachers: "I know what you are capable of. Do you?"

A turning point in my life occurred during the summer between my junior and senior years. As my senior year approached, I was both excited and apprehensive. Excited because I felt having been awarded a college scholarship, I would be allowed to start at the beginning of the school year; apprehensive because I wasn't sure that would happen.

The night before school started that September, I carefully laid out school clothes to wear the next day and polished my worn summer shoes, unaware that the next day would be one of the worst of my life.

After a sleepless night, I was awakened by Daddy's assertive voice telling Mama to get me up to go to the field. As blood rushed to my head, I began hyperventilating and struggled to pull myself to a sitting position on the side of the bed. Deep sobs followed as I was swallowed up in a void and sense of helplessness that I have never since experienced.

For weeks afterward, I went through the motions of daily life on the farm. Eating little, I lost weight from an already skinny frame. There was no place to run and hide from the sadness.

Eventually I began to feel a recognizable steely reserve returning that had been absent since that awful day. As I began to plan the next step of my life, I began to regain the hope, the strength, and the light that I was determined would not be extinguished. Knowing I would be unable to take courses required to enter college after missing two months of school, plan B began to take shape. I would attend business college in Memphis without a scholarship and work my way through school.

Sheryl Sandberg, chief operating officer of Facebook and author of *Lean In,* delivered the commencement speech at the University of California, Berkeley in May 2016. Although not to equate my experience with the tragic loss of Sheryl's husband, Dave, I could relate to many of her heartfelt comments. To quote Sheryl:

> Dave's death changed me in profound ways. I learned about the depths of sadness and the brutality of loss. But I also learned that when life sucks you under, you can kick against the bottom, break the surface, and breathe again. I learned that in the face of void—or in the face of any challenge—you can choose joy and meaning.

As of this writing, I can still feel the crushing sadness of that day. The grief I felt in later years when my dad, and then my mother, passed away, was real, as was a divorce ending my thirty-seven-year marriage and being diagnosed with breast cancer, but none of these losses affected me as deeply as did that September day in 1957.

Despite my parents' lack of understanding the importance of education, the philosophy instilled by them has served me and my two sons well. As a favorite adage goes: "It's not what you do for your children, but what you have taught them to do for themselves that will make them successful human beings." Our parents instilled in us "stuff" that lasts, and we can be grateful for that.

Life on the farm was tough, but there was no shortage of love and togetherness. I have many fond memories of growing up in a large family and benefiting from the care and wisdom of a loving mother and a hard-working father who had a tremendous sense of pride. Even today, mother's love and compassion are still with me. I feel this love and friendship all around me although she died sixteen years ago. I like to believe she left behind pieces of herself in my personality.

Speaking of my mother, one poignant memory that sticks in my mind is when we kids would get a carefully doled-out nickel to buy a candy bar or pack of gum at school. This was a great treat, and the nickel was carefully tied into the corner of a handkerchief for safekeeping; sometimes so tightly the teacher had to pick out the knot.

If you've visited an antique shop lately, you've probably come across a display of ladies' handkerchiefs common to that time. They are of every color, most often delicately trimmed with lace, but above all dainty. Contrasted with that, a poor child's handkerchief would have been a square of cotton, usually from an outgrown shirt or blouse, and then carefully hemmed by Mama's hand at home.

One day, somehow, I lost the handkerchief with my nickel in the corner. Imagine the devastating feeling of loss and the stomach-turning thought of no bite of candy I had so much looked forward to, which the nickel would've purchased that day.

At the time, I thought this may have been one of the worse things that could happen, but at this moment, I would give much to again hold in my hand one of those squares of cotton material, carefully gleaned from a not-too-faded piece of hand-me-down cloth, one with the edges still showing the needle holes and thread carefully inserted by my mother's own hand. The nickel and candy, so important at the time, eclipsed now by that desired simple square of used and faded cotton cloth.

· · · · · · · ● · · · · · · · · ·

After graduating from high school, I left the farm behind to work my way through business college. Spending mornings attending class and afternoons working to support myself, I would study far into the night to earn top grades. This may seem like an ambitious schedule but was actually the easiest my life had been. I believe it was the strenuous work on the farm and my father's teaching the dignity of hard work that prepared me for life in the big city. It instilled in me a tremendous work ethic that has been invaluable.

After graduating from college, I worked as an administrative assistant for the Tennessee Valley Authority and was later promoted to human resource officer.

During my college years, I met my future husband, Charlie, who was in his senior year at the University of Memphis. Pregnancy came shortly after the wedding, and we became parents of our first son without really having time to adjust to being married to each other. A few years later, a second son was born. For many years, I managed to raise the children, take care of the house and family, and work full time in a high-pressure managerial position with the Tennessee Valley Authority.

Both Charlie and I were pursuing professional careers, which sometimes led to long periods of separation. This further strained an already vulnerable marriage. After both sons graduated from college and made successful lives for themselves, our thirty-seven-year marriage ended in divorce. That same year my beloved mother passed away, and I was diagnosed with breast cancer. I was distressed and depressed, but my determination never wavered.

In 1996, I accepted an early retirement package from TVA, thinking my work life was complete. However, I was fortunate to be offered a position with FedEx in Memphis, where I spent fourteen years before retiring from a job I loved. I am now enjoying retirement to the fullest—embracing the joy of just being. I am thankful for broken roads I have traveled. These roads have led me to a paved path of happiness, and I am truly thankful for that.

· · · · · · · ●●●● ● ●●●● · · · · · ·

(Clara being presented Dale Carnegie "Golden Key Award for Highest Achievement")

In 2012, I was pleasantly surprised to receive the prestigious "Golden Key Award for Highest Achievement" by the Dale Carnegie School. The award is the highest given by the organization.

The following year, Dale Carnegie Official Pablo Pereyra sent the following message: "Clara, at a Dale Carnegie graduation last night, you came to mind when I gave this year's Highest Award for Achievement. Please forgive me, but I could not keep myself from sharing with those in attendance the powerful image you presented of longing to be a rider on that yellow school bus so many years ago, and your journey with an unquenchable thirst for knowledge and learning."

Pereyra went on to say: "As a previous recipient of this award, just wanted to tell you your life inspired us all. Doing the right thing, even one small gain at a time, can overcome great mountains. Be encouraged, you are riding far greater coat tails than that distant yellow bus!"

· · · · · · ●●● ● ●●●●●●● · · · ·

Statistics tell us that kids who started out like me will likely face a grim future. I could have failed high school. I could have given in to the anger and resentment I felt during my senior year. That is the real story of my life and is one of the reasons I wrote this book. I want people to know what it feels like to nearly give up on yourself. I want people to understand what happens in the lives of the poor and the impact being poor has on their children. I want people to understand what it takes to accomplish the American dream. I want people to understand that for those of us lucky enough to live the American dream.

Through writing this book, I hope to encourage people of all cultures to strive for a better life by encouraging them to practice the three *R*'s: Responsibility, respect, and restraint while trying to instill the personal strength to make wise choices. It is my deepest hope and desire that by revealing my own life story, others might grow and benefit from my experiences and accomplishments.

I am thankful for the many opportunities God has given in my life and for how He has allowed me to spread my wings through writing. Writing is my way of telling my story—one of hope, life, and love. I am also thankful for the blessings of family and friends, and for the privilege of living in a country where the daughter of a sharecropper can achieve the American dream.

· · · · · · ●●●●●● ● ●●●●● · · · · ·

As a teenager, I remember watching the movie *Blackboard Jungle* and thinking I was glad I didn't live in New York City, where gangs and disrespect for authority were rampant. In my family, upholding the family name was a deterrent to bad behavior, and we knew our parents could be relied on to support corrective measures of others in authority.

Growing up, we were molded by our parents, family, teachers, friends, and faith. As parents today, the behaviors we choose to reward and encourage will be the next generation's future.

How times have changed. In today's world, failure is the fault of someone else. Respect for authority, self, and others is considered an antiquated idea. Having children outside of marriage is flaunted by celebrities and supported by our welfare system.

I believe the core problems are only solvable by reverting to the standards based on our heritage that have served us well (i.e., two-parent families, personal responsibility, respect for others, respect for authority, respect for the law, and, most importantly, respect for ourselves).

Memphis-Arkansas Bridge spanning Mississippi
River with Memphis skyline in foreground

*Chapter 1*

# MEMPHIS AND CRIME

Let us get together in this beautiful city. Let no man, no woman, no child feel unwanted, unloved, uncared for.
—Mother Teresa, Memphis Mid-South
Coliseum, 1989

Life is precious. Life is short. At my stage of life, that's maybe a little easier to say and believe than it once was. But I count that as a blessing. Not everyone makes it to their—well—mature years. I also consider it a blessing that I live in this friendly and welcoming area called Greater Memphis.

We're not perfect, of course, because no city is. We have many of the same challenges other big cities have. But we also have true spirit. Memphis, once called the "City of Good Abode," is a good place to live, full of vibrant neighborhoods. Or it once was. When I first moved to Memphis over fifty years ago, the town was beautiful and very clean, earning the nation's Cleanest City award numerous times.

Memphis, a great city with great needs, still has many beautiful areas, but the rising violent-crime rate has helped push the city past the tipping point. Crime, poverty, and the educational system are serious issues. These are long-term problems that will take generations to solve. Numerous programs are in place to meet these challenges, but, unfortunately, family dysfunctional issues are generally not part of the discussion.

Complicating a solution is the fact that these issues are interrelated. Crime is primarily related to poverty, and poverty is most often due to a failed education, among other factors. The government's solution to these problems is new programs designed to reduce crime: job training, more benefits to single-parent recipients, and huge investments in new and better schools.

Usually missing from these discussions are the family issues related to these problems. Research has proven time and again that higher poverty and crime rates and lower educational achievement occur in families with single parents. This doesn't mean every single-parent family has these issues, but the chances are greater that an environment for children that is lacking examples and role models to mold a child in the proper direction will have these issues.

· · · · · ●●●●●●●●●●● · · · · ·

On March 3, 2008, a horrific scene was discovered in the Binghampton neighborhood of Memphis. After receiving a phone call from a concerned relative, Memphis police entered a home at 722 Lester Street to check on its occupants. What they found was shocking even to seasoned officers. The bodies of six people, ranging in age from two to thirty-three, were scattered throughout the house. In addition, three children were found seriously injured. The murder victims were identified as

Cecil Dotson, age thirty
Cecil Dotson II, age two
Cemario Dotson, age four
Shindri Roberson, age twenty-two
Hollis Seals, age thirty-three
Marisea Williams, age twenty-seven

The injured were identified as

Cecil Dotson Jr., age nine
Cedric Dotson, age five
Ceniyah Dotson, age four months

Although it took some time to sort out, autopsy reports eventually showed that the adult victims were shot multiple times, while the children were stabbed multiple times and suffered blunt force trauma to the head as the result of being beaten. The surviving victims also had stab wounds; one was found with a knife still stuck in his head.

As the community reeled from the shock of the discovery, rumors ran rampant regarding the possible motivation and the perpetrator of such a crime. For several days, consensus was that the murders must have been gang related. After all, who else would stoop to such brutality?

With this line of reasoning in mind, it was particularly disturbing when police announced just days after the murders that they had arrested and charged Jessie Dotson, age thirty-three, with the crime. He was the older brother of victim Cecil Dotson. Jessie was also the uncle of all the children involved. According to an account by one of the survivors of the massacre and a confession by Dotson himself, Jessie shot Cecil during an argument. He then attempted to kill everyone else in the house to eliminate any witnesses.

Cecil Dotson Jr. was left to die in a bathtub with a knife sticking out of his skull. After a miraculous recovery, he testified in court in October 2010 that his uncle was the one who attacked him in a rampage that left six people dead, including his parents and two siblings. When prosecutors asked where the man was who stabbed him, the boy pointed to "Uncle Junior," defendant Jessie Dotson, and softly said, "Right there."[1] Cecil Dotson Jr. testified that he was in his sister's room when he heard gunshots. He then saw his uncle pointing a gun at his father. "I saw sparks and smoke come out of the gun," he said. When the boy tried to call police, he said his uncle accosted him. "He stabbed me through my head," he said.[2]

Jessie pleaded not guilty to six first-degree murder charges and three counts of attempted first-degree murder. Authorities said Jessie, who previously served prison time for murder and was released about seven months before the killings, confessed to police days after the bodies were found. Defense attorneys contended that the killings were done by angry gang members and that the boy's testimony was unreliable because of inconsistencies and the trauma he suffered.

A Tennessee jury sentenced to death on Tuesday, October 12, 2010, a convicted killer responsible for what has been called the worst mass murder in the history of Memphis.

The case made national headlines after it appeared on TV's A&E network. The jury for this highly publicized case was selected in Nashville, Tennessee, and brought to Memphis.

Jessie Dotson first went to prison at the age of nineteen. He served fourteen years for killing a man over a drug deal. Dotson's mother, Priscilla Shaw, said he was never the same after that.

Jessie Dotson will pay the ultimate price for his crimes. I don't believe he was born evil. Jessie was the product of an environment of violence, where gang life is more common than a productive job. Yes, some people manage to rise above it, but the odds against that are great. In the end, when Jessie testified for himself, there was rage and pain. This is all he had ever known and was the only way he knew to act.

The Dotson murders may be an extreme example of crime and violence in the city of Memphis, but only because of the number of murders and stabbings occurring at the same time. Sadly, the numbers of homicides and violence-related injuries that occur over a one-week period are likely to total about the same. The citizens of Memphis are paying a high price and will continue to do so as our reputation for violence has increased.

According to the Memphis's *Commercial Appeal*, the state of Tennessee has the dubious distinction of having one of the worst violent crime rates in the United States. It is among the top in the country for homicides and robberies, and is first for aggravated assaults.

Tennessee's violent streak is concentrated in Memphis, where the violent crime rate is the country's fifth worse. Like other states with high violent-crime rates, poverty in Tennessee is widespread. This is especially true in west Tennessee, where more than 80 percent of births are to out-of-wedlock mothers. In an interview with a Memphis doctor, I was told it was closer to 85 percent.

Violence against, and by, young people is a national issue. Memphians may sometimes feel we are alone battling youth violence, but we are not. It is quickly becoming a public health crisis as real as the yellow fever epidemic once was.

Violence is a crippling public health scourge, destroying cities across America by creating an environment of fear and terror. This, in turn, affects economic growth and increases government costs from investigation, arraignment, and incarceration of offenders ... and perpetuating the cycle of crime and violence. America jumped from five hundred thousand in 1980 to 2.2 million imprisoned individuals today. Our nation leads the world in incarceration rates.[3]

In a recent weekend in Memphis, fourteen young African Americans were wounded by other blacks, most critically in eight incidents. Injuries were caused by gunshots and stabbings. Sadly, the number of Memphis homicides has reached an astounding 228 for 2016.

Civil rights activist and African American Fred Davis is the man behind this message.

A billboard in the inner-city Memphis neighborhood of Orange Mound gives new meaning to the phrase "Black Lives Matter." Big and bold, in red and black, the message stands out to drivers near the intersection of Airways Boulevard and Lamar Avenue. Civil rights activist and African American Fred Davis is the man behind this message. Davis's billboard is directly in front of his insurance company. He said he is expounding on the Black Lives Matter movement following the deaths of black men across the country resulting from black-on-black crime.

Davis said it's time black people realize they need to stop violence against each other. "We're going to have to wake up. We're going to have to say to ourselves that black lives matter, and we're going to have to refrain from killing each other out of our own frustration."

Davis accompanied Dr. Martin Luther King Jr. on his final march in Memphis. He served as the first African American chairman on the Memphis City Council. "I can speak, not from reading a book about the history, because I was a part of the history," Davis said. "I think that gives me a license as an experienced observer to push and to advocate to the black community—let's stop it."[4]

A new exhibit at the National Civil Rights Museum in downtown Memphis features the letters KKK, but it's not about what you might think. The name of the exhibit is "Kin Killin' Kin." It features charcoal paintings by African American artist James Pate and was created to call attention to black-on-black crime. "We, as black people, have put the Ku Klux Klan out of business because we are doing their work for them by terrorizing our own neighborhoods and causing a lot of strife, pain and suffering through black-on-black crime,"[5] Pate said.

Mr. Pate and Mr. Davis are to be commended for their brave expressions of this tragic trend in our community.

After a mob of young black teens attacked a white teen employee in the parking lot of a midtown Kroger grocery, leaving him with serious injuries, a local TV station decided to ask some of the black teens what can be done to stop such violence. Their answer: "nothing." Two of the teens, who only gave nicknames, told the reporter they thought the Kroger mob attack "was fun."

"That's just what kids do, our generation, I mean," one of the teens said. When the reporter asked, "Why do you think these kids are drawn to that violence?" the other responded. "It's fun."

"Nobody cares about jail," the men said, laughing. "You go in, and you get out. If you don't get out, you're in with people you know."

When the TV reporter showed former Memphis Mayor A. C. Wharton, an African American, the interview, he was disgusted by what he called a flippant attitude toward the violent attack. "There's absolutely no excuse," he said.

Mayor Wharton said there are options out there. "We have a summer jobs program. All those things need to be expanded. If you've been in trouble before, we have reentry programs that will help you clean up your act and expunge the violation from your record," he said.

But the men countered, "Why would I break my neck for $300 every two weeks when I can make $300 a night off one serve? Speaking for the robbers, you can make that in a minute or two."

As for federal- and state-funded community programs and after-school activities planned by the city, the men said, "It's boring. That's how people look at it. It's boring. The image with the drugs and the violence and guns and fighting and all that … it looks fun. That's what people see. They see fun."

The teens told the reporter that to change that mind-set, they need to see more people turning away from the culture of gang life. While they say some older generation gang members are doing that, many still push them to live the street life.[6]

The astounding fact is that more youths die from homicide each year than from cancer, heart disease, birth defects, flu and pneumonia, respiratory diseases, stroke, and diabetes combined, according to a 2011 CDC report called "Preventing Youth Violence: Opportunities for Action."

The problem is particularly high among African Americans in large urban centers such as Memphis, where poverty and a lack of educational achievement are breeding grounds for gangs.

That same CDC report said the murder rate among black teens and young men ages ten to twenty-four was about twenty-nine for every one hundred thousand individuals, which was nearly fourteen times higher than the rate for white youth, the overwhelming number of which were black-on-black crime.

There have been over four thousand murders in the city of Chicago alone since Barak Obama was elected president. Over 90 percent of these murders were black-on-black crimes. Very seldom do any of these murders make national news. Do these black lives mean nothing to the Black Lives Matter (BLM) organizers?

Take the tragic story of Phyllis Gray. For the fourth time in her life, Phyllis recently got the news that another child had been gunned down in Washington, DC. Phyllis says she is "emotionally drained—tired of the calls, tired of the funerals, tired of the T-shirts bearing the faces of her four dead sons."

As the nation's top brass, tycoons, lawmakers, and the famous gathered only a couple of miles away to celebrate the opening of the National Museum of African American History and Culture, Phyllis was stuck in a well-known cycle in her neighborhood: violence, silence—violence, silence.

The first time she was a distraught mother was in 2001 when her son Samuel Phillips, twenty-three, was shot and killed in a halfway house. Prior to the beginning of his trial, another son, Demetrius, one of the witnesses for the prosecution, was killed. On a bitterly cold November night in 2004, her third son, Carlos was killed. And then, there was another call last month. Her fourth son, Scorpio-Rodney was shot and killed when two men pulled up to a barbecue outing and shot their guns into the crowd. Nine people were hit by gunfire, and two of them died, including Scorpio. No one has been held accountable for any of her son's murders. Phyllis wonders aloud: "Four of my sons have been killed, and no one has gone to jail. Do their lives matter?"

On the off chance that black lives truly mattered to the BLM organization, would they not be as vocal about the thousands of blacks who are being slaughtered by other blacks as they are a life that is taken by a policeman they think may be racist? The dismal truth is that publicizing black-on-black crime does not fit the political agenda. My heart breaks for the families of these victims. As a mother, I can only imagine the pain they must feel.

How much pain, how much cruelty! Is it possible that brothers and sisters created in God's image are capable of doing this to each other? Fellow Americans, this is not Auschwitz or our fallen war heroes ... this is happening in the United States of America! Every human life is precious and must be protected.
—Pope Francis

The Brennan Center Law and Policy Institute in New York said in a recent examination of crime occurring in large urban areas last year that just three cities—Baltimore, Chicago and Washington DC—accounted for more than half of the overall increase in homicides in the country's twenty-five biggest cities. Chicago police have said that the greater part of the increases in violence there are driven by gang members using unlawful weapons, and that it is, to a great extent, concentrated in areas in the city's south and west sides.

We have only to multiply the number of murders in Chicago by the number of cities in our nation with a large inner-city population to see the crisis facing our country. Many believe this is a greater threat to our nation than ISIS.

And since we are talking numbers, let's look at two recent homicides in Memphis. On April 22, 2016, a seventeen-year-old young man was gunned down on a playground while other young, innocent children were playing nearby. Two days later, a fifteen-year-old girl who was with a group of friends at the Foote Homes public housing project near downtown Memphis was shot and killed in a drive-by shooting. Her death brought total homicides for the first four months of 2016 to eighty-five—compared to forty-five for the same time last year. As the year wore on, homicides continued to increase at an alarming rate, ending 2016 with an astounding record of 228 murders.

The median age of those arrested on murder charges so far this year is twenty-six, with the youngest being a twelve-year-old child. These and other homicides leave people questioning the mind-set of those individuals who would take an innocent life just to settle a personal feud.

Yes, 228 murders in one year should equal a public health crisis and state of emergency in anyone's book. It's not just Memphis—other major metropolitan areas are dealing with the same crisis. Memphis is not alone in seeing a surge in killings this year.

For the second consecutive year, the number of homicides increased in 2016 in more than two dozen major US cities. The numbers were particularly dismal for some places—Chicago, Los Angeles, Dallas, Detroit, Las Vegas, and Memphis—where the number of murders increased in the first few months after killings and other violent crimes also went up in 2015.

"I was very worried about it last fall, and I am more worried because the numbers are not only going up, they're continuing to go up in most cities faster than they were going up last year," FBI Director James B. Comey said. "Something is happening."

Criminologists and law enforcement authorities, including Comey, say they are unsure of the reasons for the increases. They offer some conceivable explanations, including gang violence and bloodshed stemming from drug usage. "I don't know what the answer is, but, holy cow, do we have a problem," Comey said.

During his remarks, Comey said he was worried about this being a problem most people can drive around. As examples, he said that on Chicago's Magnificent Mile or the Las Vegas Strip, people may not be as aware of the killings in other parts of the cities. "It's happening in certain parts of the cities, and the people dying are almost entirely Black and Latino men."[7]

It is no surprise that the areas of the cities affected by these high crime rates have a large percentage of poor families with single mothers heading the households. How many children are being raised in these parts of the cities with no father figure in the home? How many of these single mothers are struggling to make ends meet whether they are on welfare or have jobs that don't allow them the time they need to care for their children? How many families in these parts of the cities depend on the government, not to get them through a tough time, but as a way of life in generation after generation? Mr. Comey and other experts may find the common denominator for this tragic dilemma by answering these questions.

Many people believe the "politically correct cover-up" is one of the reasons for our high crime rate. I wholeheartedly agree with Dr. Ben Carson in his recent statement that "America has gone mad with political correctness which is destroying our society."

Neither the CDC nor the police, nor anyone else, has made improvements in this national dilemma that work long term. Those bent on committing violent acts against others care little at the time about the consequences of their brutality. Additional police and longer prison terms will not help either. Reducing the allure of young teenagers to join gangs and helping families in poverty with better parenting skills is essential but does not address the root of the problem. Discouraging the allure of teenagers having babies out of wedlock, which leads to poverty and crime, is the primary solution to the problem. It is the common thread that binds together thousands of families that live in poverty.

With over two hundred homicides in 2016, deadly black-on-black crime is real and is reaching epidemic stage in Memphis alone. Unless the entire community gets involved in discouraging this lifestyle, it threatens to drag our city down the drain. And until we address these issues, all other efforts to control our explosive violent crime rate are doomed to long-term failure.

A close friend I will call Frank ran a successful automotive business in South Memphis for many years. As the culture in the area began to change, he dealt with break-ins and robberies on a frequent basis. Frank was eventually forced to close his business after being the victim of twenty-seven robberies in his last year of operation. When he asked local police what would happen if he shot one of the intruders, Frank was told he would be arrested and go to jail.

In the 1930s and 1940s, many people, black and white, lived in real poverty with no government help, and yet the number of single-parent households was a fraction of today's number. In the 1960s, demeaning segregation hampered progress, yet illegitimacy was only one-third of today's number. This is a multiethnic populace issue. It is not because Memphis is predominately black that there is a problem. Any woman or group or any society that allows men to walk away from family responsibilities scot-free is in trouble.

The ACLU and the far left have been effective in removing the traditional moral influence from the public. The federal government has succeeded through welfare programs in empowering, if not encouraging, generations of single-parent families.

Those who are in influential positions such as religious leaders, educators, lawmakers, parents, etc., should speak for the time-honored reinstatement of values of morality such as education, hard work, and government independence, as well as respect for self and others. It would be amazing if we saw this kind of passion when our children are being shot and killed.

Take the story of a fifteen-year-old child who evaded transfer to adult court amid a Shelby County (Memphis) Juvenile Court hearing despite confessing to shooting two people outside a home. That's because his defense attorney effectively argued that his client had been brought up in an environment that encourages striking back and violence—accusing the teen's thirty-year-old mother of dropping off her son near the crime scene to settle a score she had with a woman who lived there.

"His mother was basically using this child to settle her problems with others," his lawyer said. The judge told the mother she bore some blame for her son's criminal act. He ordered the youth removed from her home and placed in the guardianship of the State Department of Children's Services until he is nineteen. The teen's lawyer said he faced a daunting challenge keeping his client in the juvenile system because the teen admitted to police he shot into a group, striking two people in the legs.

"The court did an incredible job peeling back the layers and looking at this child's social history as well as the absence of parental direction and his environment,"[8] the attorney said. Sadly, this is an all too common scenario affecting hundreds of young men and women in the Memphis area.

The case of Cartrail Robertson tells a sad but common story of children in peril in the Memphis area: fatherless young men who are lured into a dangerous world of guns and violence and confused identities. The thirteen-year-old young man posted his picture on Facebook depicting his wannabe thug lifestyle just hours before being shot and killed by a fifteen-year-old.

"Cartrail was absolutely at odds about his identity without a doubt," said Kenny Stubblefield, director of Memphis Athletic Ministries. Cartrail, seemingly seeking that identity, was a regular participant at the athletic ministry for years. "He was a brilliant kid, incredibly observant; had all the potential in the world. But with the environment he grew up in, with guns and drugs all around, what's accepted as cool is a gangster kind of violent persona. I don't think he lived that lifestyle, but he definitely felt a need to present himself that way, especially to his peers,"[9] said Stubblefield.

Delvin Lane is a fatherless former drug dealer and former gang leader in Memphis. Lane didn't know Cartrail, but he sees kids like him every day. "Older men prey on fatherless boys who are eleven, twelve, thirteen," said Lane, a community violence prevention supervisor for former Mayor A. C. Wharton's Anti-Violence Gun Down Initiative. "Kids that age are old enough to start wanting some power and control over their lives, but still young enough to be vulnerable and manipulated. Older guys start acting like their daddy, giving them love, attention and protection they never experienced in their home,"[10] said Lane.

Cartrail's biological father has been in prison for ten years. His mother, Elonda, a single welfare mother, just had her thirteenth child. Said Lane, "He was heartbroken, missing his father all these years and I think he was lonely. I think someone out there started acting like his daddy. I think he found a second family that wasn't good for him."

Take the cases of seven-year old Kirsten Williams and fifteen-year-old Cateria Stokes, who were both killed in drive-by shootings the same night last year in Memphis. The pretty seven-year-old girl was playing in her driveway after school. The fifteen-year-old girl was asleep in her bedroom in the middle of the night. Both were shot and killed the same night in separate parts of town in what police have said were drive-by shootings.

The cases of Cateria and Kirsten's shocking deaths do not end there. Cateria's single mother has now lost three of her children to gun violence, and one is in jail on murder charges. Cameron Stokes, the older sibling of Cateria, was shot to death at The Hamlets condominiums not long after Cateria's death. Cameron and another man were found murdered inside an automobile in that same Memphis neighborhood.

Chasity Stokes, the sister of Cateria and Cameron, said she's tired of attending funerals, tired of showing pictures of her siblings killed by gunfire, and she is tired of trying to make sense of tragedy. "Now my brother is gone—another brother gone,"[11] Chasity said. Cameron is her mother's third child killed by gun violence, and she has another son sitting in jail charged with murdering Kirsten. The Stokes family said they are living in fear and dread, wondering who will be next.

Kirsten Williams and Cateria Stokes are two more victims of our unending and unconscionable inability to stop young men, in particular, from killing each other. Former Mayor, A. C. Wharton called for more "thug control … for these despicable people who seek to bring fear and violence to our communities." The African American police chief called for automatic life sentences for "those thugs who decide to pick up a gun and carry out a crime, especially if it results in taking a young life."

Former Mayor Wharton was the county's public defender for more than twenty years. African American Toney Armstrong, who at that time was police director, was a member of the Memphis Police Department for more than twenty-five years. "We can hear their outrage and frustration—and why not," says David Waters, columnist for the Memphis *Commercial Appeal*. "Those two men worked tirelessly to get young men to stop shooting at each other." [12]

Wharton and Armstrong long championed youth education projects, summer jobs programs, jail diversion projects, gang intervention instruction, community safety programs, and religious programs. No doubt all of those efforts—along with the tireless work of others in the criminal justice system and philanthropic organizations helped to keep the criminal activity from getting even worse.

Be that as it may, why, with all these programs and the possibility of arrest, conviction, and incarceration, does this not keep young men from killing each other? That's an even larger and more challenging task.

According to Webster's dictionary, a thug is a violent person, particularly a criminal. As described by the late rapper Tupac Shakur, a thug is a person who has nothing and, therefore, has nothing to lose. "I didn't choose the thug life; the thug life chose me," Shakur, the millionaire hip-hop entertainer, told an interviewer not long before he was murdered in 1996. Said Shakur, "All I'm trying to do is survive and make good out of the dirty, nasty, unbelievable lifestyle that they gave me."

In other words, a thug is a product of his surroundings—most often one that is fatherless, poor, jobless, and feels hopeless. "Violence holds it all together," said African American minister the Reverend Marlon Foster, who grew up, lives in, and works in mostly black South Memphis. "It's how you get what you need. It's how you protect yourself, how you keep others from taking what you have, including what little self-respect you might have or want."[13]

In an environment where gangs are the only employers, illegal drugs are the only reliable source of income (other than government benefits), and violence is an occupational hazard, going to jail isn't a deterrent; it's a job transfer. It's an environment where vicious retaliation is another form of "thug control." Being seen as weak, or allowing one to be disrespected or taken advantage of, is worse than the threat of jail or a graveyard.

Gun violence isn't just a response; it's an action that begins with a fight or a real or imagined slight that escalates. It's an environment with ready access to firearms. The individuals breaking into our homes, businesses, and cars aren't simply looking for money. According to the Bureau of Justice Statistics, most guns used in crimes have been stolen or unlawfully exchanged from legitimate gun owners.

Almost two hundred thousand firearms are stolen each year in America. More than sixteen hundred weapons have been stolen in Memphis alone in each of the previous two years—half in home robberies and a quarter from motor vehicles.[14]

"Put a gun in the hands of someone with little or no impulse control, or someone who feels like they have nothing to lose, and it's the wild, wild, west," Rev. Foster said. Foster isn't opposed to "gun control." But he would like to see more emphasis on "thug control." His South Memphis ministry, known as Knowledge Quest, hosted one of the first Universal Parenting Places (UPP) in Memphis. The UPPs are the first result of the ACE Task Force. ACE stand for adverse childhood experiences, which include violence, abuse, neglect, and family dysfunction.

Brain research shows that prolonged exposure to frequent and destructive trauma, such as violence and neglect in the home, and living in a violent neighborhood overloads a young mind's defense systems and impairs normal child development. Those negative childhood experiences can appear months and years later in the form of irresponsible, reckless, and criminal behaviors that turn fights or slights into gun battles. Says Rev. Foster, "Many efforts have the unfortunate task of mopping up spills, but we have to cut off the faucet of violence. Thug control, which is necessary, is aimed at the lawless. Thug prevention, no less important, will require us to address the fatherless, the jobless and the hopeless."

A local acquaintance with a gun carry permit related a story that happened to him recently. He was at a Memphis grocery, and a little boy behind him saw a pistol poking out of his holster and asked him why he carried a gun. "To stop the bad guys," he mumbled. But the sad truth is that he carried the pistol because Memphis's inner city is a dangerous place. Children are abandoned to be raised by their grandparents or other relatives. We have "baby daddys" and "baby mamas" instead of mothers and fathers. The little boy at the grocery has a better chance of going to prison than he does of attending college.

Take the case of Terrance Lewis, who was sentenced to prison for killing one person and wounding five others in a neighborhood shootout in Memphis. When it was his turn to talk at his trial, Lewis took the witness stand and declared, "I'm a product of my environment. I had a gun because I live in South Memphis."[15]

The shooting occurred when a kid threw a firecracker at another during a holiday get-together in South Memphis. At first appearing to be gunshots, the firecracker incident sparked a riot among more than a dozen adults. Lewis said he began firing his gun during the brawl to defend his sister. When the smoke from the guns and fireworks cleared, one person was dead and five others were wounded, including a seventy-seven-year-old woman and a ten-year-old boy.

Lewis, who was sentenced to ninety-four years in prison, said he was the son of a single welfare mother with four other children and that growing up in South Memphis forced him to quickly learn the danger of the streets and how to protect himself. He started getting in trouble at age fourteen. "There was constantly some kind of trouble going on," said Lewis, who said he first smoked pot at age ten. "Going to the wrong neighborhood could get you killed. It's territorial. It's like that in the jungle."

At age seventeen, Lewis was charged with and convicted of aggravated assault and aggravated robbery. He served most of a fifteen-year sentence. Before he went off to prison the first time, Lewis said his mother gave him a few words of advice: Always fight back, don't think too much, and don't mess with punks. Said Lewis, "I always tried to follow her advice."

Deandre Turner has seven slugs in his body. His kneecap, crushed by a gunshot wound, is plastic, and he has lost feeling in his right leg and his left hand. He has a broad scar running down the center of his stomach—a result of being shot and left for dead. In one shooting, he took thirteen shots to his middle chest. He was shot again in 2005, in both legs and in the midsection.

Deandre's life was twice spared by doctors at the Regional Medical Center in Memphis, one of the nation's leading trauma centers. When he was shot the first time, he was hospitalized for twenty days at a cost of hundreds of thousands of dollars. He is learning how to walk again. Some days he can barely stand up.

Deandre is all too mindful of how drastically his life has changed for the worse. "It's real depression," he regretfully said. "I don't want to be around people because

I'm in so much pain. I don't feel whole as a man, a father, a grandfather. I go through days when I cry. It's a miserable feeling living day-to-day in my condition, trying to live a normal life."[16]

Deandre grew up in South Memphis, where gunshots and violence were a way of life. "You adapt to your surroundings," he said, "or you become a casualty yourself." But now, having spent time in prison on an attempted murder charge and struggling to recover from devastating physical and mental injuries, he thinks of life differently. Wishing he could start over, he said, "The way I was taught was wrong; I was lied to."

Exposure to violence and trauma harms youngsters growing up in areas where homicides have become the norm. Every corner has one: a person with a slit up the center of his stomach where his internal organs were hit with bullets, and young guys in wheelchairs. For some, it is actually a medal of honor.

The pace of Memphis's murder rate is highly disturbing. Tragically, crime is now a centerpiece of our community. Daily "breaking news" on local TV newscasts is about the murder or murders occurring that day or night. A more accurate "breaking news" report would be: no murders in the city of Memphis today! The city's government and citizens seem paralyzed as to what to do about it.

We should ask ourselves, where is the outrage when we have children on our streets shot and killed? It's unfortunate we must spend so much money fighting crime and treating the injured while other communities are putting their money into making cities more livable.

Myneishia Johnson was a young lady with many titles: eighteen-year-old, soon to be high school graduate from Booker T. Washington High School (BTW); mom to a one-year-old son; basketball player; and honor roll student. She goes out one evening and winds up in a body bag as the result of a random shooting on the streets of Memphis. Myneishia is now one of more than two hundred people who were murdered last year.

Another BTW student, Quanisha Sims, 18, was shot in May of last year. Also the mother of a one-year-old, Quanisha was happily preparing for her senior prom. Police said Sims was getting a perm at her North Memphis home when her sister's boyfriend shot her. Gratefully, Quanisha survived and was out of the hospital in time to participate in her high school graduation.

Fifteen-year-old Vianca Harris was not that fortunate. Vianca, who was four to five weeks pregnant, enjoyed fashion and dancing. She was shot and killed after an altercation in the apartment of a companion.

Shortly before the shootings of Myneishia, Quanisha, and Vianca, another fifteen-year-old girl was gunned down and murdered in an apartment shootout in the Foote Homes community of Memphis.

On July 1, 2016, four precious children were fatally stabbed at a Memphis apartment complex, and their mother is in custody for their murders. Called an "egregious act of evil," by the local newspaper, it was one of the worst acts of violence in what had already been a bloody year in the Memphis area. Shanynthia Gardner is charged with four counts of first-degree murder associated with aggravated child abuse. According to Gardner's arrest affidavit, deputies found her on the scene with superficial cuts to her neck and wrists. The four children found with "severe throat lacerations," were: six-month-old Yahzi; Sya, three; Sahvi, two; and four-year-old Tallen. Seven-year-old Dallen escaped when he ran from the home yelling that his mother stabbed his sisters.

These senseless killings are just a sample of the violence that occurred in Memphis in 2016. Don't kid yourself, fellow Memphians; this is a crisis. The murder rate is out of control and impacts all of us.

Memphis *Commercial Appeal* columnist David Waters wrote a recent article entitled "Helping troubled kids before they shoot." Waters states that kids five to ten years old can be identified by teachers, counselors, and social workers as likely to become "young men with childlike emotions and adult weapons whose anger, fear and paranoia become lethal."

As Waters further states, "These kids are angrier than other kids. They have a harder time controlling their emotions and impulses. Their first protective reaction to any sort of perceived threat is to fight or lash out—verbally or physically or both. That's because their nervous systems are set, almost from birth, in trauma mode. They've been exposed to multiple traumas and chronic stress and pervasive violence. They don't know who they can trust, if anyone. They've seen their mothers, fathers, siblings, cousins, and friends get drunk, high, arrested, beaten, shot and killed, right in front of them."

If experts can identify troubled children before they become violent, can special efforts to help these children be put in place? In addition to regular classes, could a class be added to the school curriculum that teaches life skills such as anger management, communication skills, importance of going to school and completing at least a high school education, respect for others, the false sense of gang participation, and the end result of a life of crime and violence?

Charles Traughber, chairman of the Tennessee Board of Parole, sees that trouble every day. "By the time a young man gets into the Department of Children's Services or the correctional system, it's harder to turn a kid around. Someone, preferably a father figure, needs to have been involved in his life. Before school, at home, someone who is stable and working and helps a boy feel as though he is a part of something; someone who really cares and who instills values that support family or the community."[17]

In Memphis and other urban areas, chronic truancy is a precursor to poor educational achievement and a life of low-paying, dead-end jobs. The truants likely will be enticed to take part in illegal activities, leading to half of them being incarcerated by the time they are twenty years old, according to criminal justice studies. There comes a time, however, when the realities of adulthood hit, and these young men are ill prepared to deal with those realities.

The negative statistics on young black men are grim with regard to crime, homicide, incarceration, unemployment rates, and academics. The academic attainment gap between young African American men and their counterparts continues to grow.

With the record number of homicides in 2016, the year set a record for bloodshed in the city of Memphis. While the growing number of homicides has grabbed the biggest headlines, it is the hundreds of nonfatal shootings, stabbings, and beatings that really capture the magnitude of the violence that has plagued the city in recent years.

There were over four hundred nonfatal injuries caused by violence last year. Some walked out of the Med, a local hospital and trauma center, after life-saving treatment; others left in wheelchairs, some to be there permanently. Of the nonfatal domestic violence injuries treated at the Med, some survived, some are disabled, and most live in pain.

As for the economic cost of domestic violence at the Med alone, surgery for a gunshot wound costs an average of $100,000. In Memphis, where the majority of residents living in the most violent neighborhoods are poor and have no insurance, taxpayers bear the brunt of the costs. With at least two or three daily shootings, stabbings, and other violent acts leaving many in critical condition with lengthy hospital stays, the annual cost to taxpayers for indigent services resulting from violence is a conservative $1 billion!

"A bullet tears through flesh like a high-voltage missile," says Dr. Thomas Scalea of the University of Maryland Shock Trauma Center. "Once inside the body it can travel, destroying internal organs and fragmenting bone in places far from the puncture site," Scalea said.

"Spinal cord injuries from gunshot wounds are all too common; some culprits purposely shoot to paralyze not kill." For the injured, survival is just the beginning of a lifelong battle. "If you are a quadriplegic, and we spared your life, that's great—sort of," Scales said. "But your life is irrevocably changed now."[18]

For the severely injured, physical pain is only a part of the anguish that comes with being shot: Their identities and futures are forever altered, as are the lives of their families and their communities.

Children who watch the violence often have PTSD, or posttraumatic stress disorder. The kids sleep on the floor or in a bathtub because they're afraid they'll get shot if they sleep on the bed. A lot is on the line for Memphis and other urban communities—and for the taxpayers. If these children are not helped, they will likely turn to violence themselves or need psychological help paid for by the government.

Teachers in inner-city schools learn that instead of asking a misbehaving child, "What's wrong with you?" they ask, "What happened last night?" The stressed children have worsened asthma. Some need stitches from being beaten up on the way to school or at home.

For children in the inner-city neighborhoods where crime and violence are an everyday occurrence, things really never quiet down. A distant gunshot, a fight in the courtyard, a memorial of flowers, balloons, or stuffed animals remembering a homicide victim are common sights.

Have we become desensitized by violence and shootings? On a recent Memorial Day weekend, sixty-nine people were shot in Chicago. The story of a child falling into a gorilla cage in Cleveland, Ohio, had 54 percent more media coverage than did the shootings in Chicago. The city had over four hundred shootings in one month with sixty-six people killed. As of this December 2016 writing, Chicago had 762 murders for the year. Most were black-on-black crimes.[19] If we had a single event in the United States costing 762 lives, there would be wall-to-wall media coverage for weeks.

Last year, President Barack Obama gave an inspiring speech in Washington, DC, calling for action to reverse underachievement among young minority men.

The president's profoundly personal speech began his "My Brother's Keeper" initiative, intended to help young African American and Hispanic men "become better husbands and fathers and well-educated, hardworking good citizens." Obama said he made bad choices when he was young, growing up in a fatherless home, and even confessed to getting high and not considering school important. "I made excuses," he said. He added that young African American and Hispanic men have no excuses and should "tune out the naysayers who say if the deck is stacked against you, you might as well give up or settle into the stereotype."

On the same day in Memphis, officials with the Shelby County Truancy Reduction Program held an event to talk about the program and to call for more mentors to help keep young people in school.

Both occasions referenced a problem that is dogging the United States, especially its urban areas: By what means can we as a nation and community better provide hope and opportunity to a segment of the population that many perceive to be dangerous and unwilling to take advantage of opportunities that could lead them to become successful adults?

Two of the key answers to that question are: We need to quit looking at these young men as stereotypes and acknowledge there are barriers that create obstacles to success. Second, as the president focused on, these young men must be willing to help themselves by taking advantage of opportunities that will allow them to jump over those hurdles and climb the ladders of opportunity that allow individuals to get out of a life of dependency. Barriers and challenges can be overcome with hard work, education, and the right mind-set.

The reality is African American men are still dying from criminal homicides—primarily black-on-black crimes—at an alarming rate. On any given day, according to a recent national study, about 23 percent of all African American men ages sixteen to twenty-four who had dropped out of high school are in jail, prison, or a juvenile justice institution.[20]

The flip side of those numbers is that most young African American men are neither in jail nor committing crimes. Still, the percentage of those who are killing each other is out of control, with far too many people of color being killed.

Some feel it's time to stop making excuses and start demanding that the black youth of today realize their potential. Fifty years have passed since the civil rights movement created more level opportunities for black youth, and I believe Dr. Martin Luther King Jr. would be appalled at their lack of progress.

Looking at nationwide data from the FBI, homicides during 2015 totaled 15,696. With a projected increase of 3.9 percent for 2016, total homicides will reach over sixteen thousand nationally. Over 70 percent of these homicides are black-on-black crimes. These numbers are especially disturbing since the African American population comprises only 13 percent of the total US population.[21]

As 2017 dawned, the city of Memphis recorded its first homicide. Kiara Tatum, a LeMoyne-Owen College student who wanted to become a nurse, was gunned down in her front yard.

The previous day, at a New Year's Eve prayer breakfast, Memphis Mayor Jim Strickland and former Mayor Dr. Willie Herenton set the tone for the meeting. "This is our problem," Herenton said. "We've got to be fathers to these young men who have no fathers."

As columnist David Waters states in the same article, "The last day of 2016 might be the most important day in 2017 for Memphis, the day we decided to get real about crime and violence and our responsibilities as adults to the children in this community. The day we confessed that even good and functional government is, at best, a poor substitute for good parents and functional homes.

The day we acknowledged that more police officers, preachers, teachers, and social workers can't replace the transformative power of personal responsibility and personal relationships."

As Memphis citizens, we should all resolve not to allow our record homicide rate to become accepted as the new normal. Every violent death is a death in a family, a cause for grief, and a motivation to create a more peaceful city.

# Chapter 2

# MEMPHIS AND TEEN PREGNANCY

Some may say we are being insensitive and picking on single mothers. That is certainly *not* the case. We are not picking on fifteen thousand single mothers. The focus is on the children and the consequences of being born to a single mother.

Memphis has an abundance of single-parent households living in poverty. Nearly half of Memphis's children under eighteen live in poverty. Some 60 percent of births are to single mothers. Such a family environment can discourage success. As a result, the cycle of poverty and crime continues through more generations.

Statistics on the costs to Memphis and to taxpayers of young women having babies too soon are staggering. Dr. David Ciscel, an economics professor recently retired from the University of Memphis, has released his estimate on what too much teen pregnancy means to the city. He did his report for Memphis Teen Vision, a coalition of fifty groups trying to cope with various aspects of teen pregnancy.

This year, according to Ciscel's work, about twenty-two hundred teenage girls will have babies in Shelby County, which includes Memphis. These are mothers ages ten to nineteen. More than 80 percent of these babies will be born to moms who are not married. Most of the pregnancies will be unintended.

Only 28 percent of teen mothers in Memphis have a high school diploma, another 9 percent have some college, and 63 percent have less than a high school education.[22] Consequently, the potential that these young women will be economically self-sufficient is low. In addition, a quarter of teenage mothers in Memphis have a second child during their teenage years.

The high teen birth rate in the Greater Memphis area comes with a huge price tag. Who pays it? The answer, of course, is that we all do—the teen moms themselves, their children, the taxpayers, our schools, our employers, and our communities. Most studies on the costs of teen pregnancy emphasize the public (taxpayer) funds spent helping a pregnant teenager and her child. In Shelby County, the public costs can range into the millions of dollars annually depending on what is added into the equation. To get a fuller picture, it is necessary to factor in the negative economic impact of early childbearing on a woman's lifetime earning capacity.

Despite a slight decline in teen pregnancies over the past two years, the Memphis/Shelby County metropolitan area still has one of the highest rates of teen pregnancy and births in the nation. Programs such as A Step Ahead and CHOICES are working to decrease the number of teen births.

The initial costs of teenage pregnancy include prenatal care, physician's services, and the costs of hospital delivery. However, the actual cost of delivery is small compared to the cost of raising a child. A regular hospital delivery costs over $5,000 in hospital and physician costs. This adds up to over $20 million for all the teenage births in Shelby County the past year.

For the first three years of her child's life, a teenage mother is usually a single person. Early childhood costs include all of the costs of raising the child during these first three years. For a low-income single parent, this average cost for the first three years is over $34,000, mostly in indigent care paid for by taxpayers. That includes delivery, housing, clothing, health care, food, and child care.[23]

Teen pregnancy, particularly combined with problems of poverty, poor education, and weak family structure, can result in a lifetime of poor economic performance for a young woman. Lack of appropriate skills to get, to hold, and to advance in a job have been problems in the region for a long time. And those continue to be problems.

A significant minority of Shelby County workers do not earn a living wage—enough income to be self-sufficient without public assistance. Teenage pregnancy contributes to the low-wage problem significantly. Today's job market requires skills, skills that often require a community college or university education. Postponing the acquisition of these skills increases the probability that the skills won't be acquired at all.

Because most teen mothers don't finish high school, their lost earnings reach $125,000 by the time they are age twenty-four, compared with young women who finish high school and college.

Over the course of her entire work life, a woman who begins adulthood as a teen mother loses about $410,000 in earnings by not completing a high school diploma, $980,000 by not getting an associate's degree, and $1,500,000 by not obtaining a bachelor's degree. And that is for one teen mother in Shelby County. Multiplying those figures by the number of local teen mothers shows us that the Memphis economy is losing millions of dollars in productivity every year to teen pregnancies.

Nationally, the annual public cost of teen childbearing is over $12 billion for the more than five hundred thousand births for teens nineteen years old and younger. The breakdown in public costs is $2.8 billion in public health care costs, $3.6 billion in child welfare costs, $3.1 billion in additional incarceration costs, and $3.2 billion in lost taxes (due to lower earned incomes).[24]

One result of teenage pregnancy is women earning less, which is followed by women spending less on themselves and on supporting their children into adulthood. Women who do not have the funds to raise the next generation of children are likely to repeat the cycle of poverty that leads to educational failure and job instability. In many cases, the intergenerational cycle of teenage pregnancy will repeat itself twelve to fifteen years later.

There have been many studies of the issues surrounding teenage pregnancy. Evidence suggests that teen pregnancies exacerbate other existing conditions such as household poverty and high incidence of crime. Teenage pregnancies are associated with increased job instability and lower earnings for the mothers. Teenage pregnancies often result in children who will also be trapped in a lifetime cycle of poverty, poor educational attainment, and weak job prospects. Daughters of teen moms are three times more likely to become teen mothers themselves, and sons of teen moms are more than twice as likely to end up in prison.

Teenage mothers tend to come from family backgrounds where poverty is the norm, where job stability is low, and where education is not a first priority of early life.

Consequently, teenage pregnancy often continues a cycle of deprivation—transferring social and economic problems of one generation to the next generation. On average, teen mothers also tend to come from social environments where other factors—poverty, lack of education, abuse, and absence of a father figure in the home—also tend to increase reliance on public assistance in order to progress through life.

Eighty percent of human brain development occurs from the time of conception to age three. It is during this period in which children born to single mothers are most likely to be deprived of adequate prenatal care, the nurturing of a two-parent home environment, and to suffer from factors that result from poverty.

Today, 94 percent of the children living in poverty in Memphis live with single mothers. This revolving cycle of poverty is at the root of Memphis's problems in education, crime, and unemployment. Many such babies likely are the third, fourth, or even fifth generations of children born to single mothers living in poverty. In other words, this has been a recurring problem in Memphis for many decades.

There has developed in Memphis an attitude of resignation about this issue and a lifestyle that is inconsistent with good education and good economic success. The results of this lifestyle no longer are merely personal problems. They have become public problems because they have been major factors in pushing Memphis past the tipping point. For the first time in a century Memphis has lost population while virtually all other major southern cities continue to grow.

For approximately twenty-two hundred girls and young women each year in Memphis, pregnancy forever changes their financial prospects in a negative way. Will some of these women overcome the barriers to their own financial self-sufficiency and success? Although the answer may be yes for a few highly determined and fortunate individuals, the overall picture is bleak. The women, the children, and the society that cares for them will feel its effects for decades to come.

The Economic Impact of Teen Pregnancy
in Memphis/Shelby County, Tennessee
By David H. Ciscel, emeritus professor of economics

The University of Memphis[25]

The Public Costs of Teen Pregnancy
- $5 billion in taxpayer money in 2015.
- Public assistance funds over half the cost for the first 13 years of the child's life.
- Over half of teen mothers do not have a high school diploma.
- Many teen mothers have difficulty completing job training.

Characteristics of Teen Pregnancy in Memphis, Tennessee
- In 2014, there were 14,409 live births in Shelby County
- 2,181 of these babies were born to mothers aged 10 to 19
- Over 80 percent were unintended pregnancies
- Almost all were to unmarried mothers
- Immediate Cost/Benefit Ratio
- Costs to deliver a child for a teenager = $4,688
- Investment for contraception = $267 per year

Early Childhood Cost/Benefit Ratio
- Three-year cost to raise a child in Memphis = $33,344
- Investment for contraception = $800 for three years

Early Pregnancy and the Earnings Gap
- Impairs educational progress
- Slows job skill development

- Results in dependence on public assistance
- Reduces earning capacity life long

- Comparative Woman's Earnings (Starting yearly incomes)
- No high school diploma        $ 6,657
- High school only              $13,070
- Associate's degree            $17,327
- Bachelor's degree             $22,052

Lost Earning Capacity to Age 24
- $51,304 without a high school diploma
- $85,352 without an associate's degree
- $123,160 without a bachelor's degree

- A Lifetime of Lost Earning Capacity
- No high school diploma        $410,064
- No associates degree          $908,192
- No bachelor's degree          $1,400,820

· · · · · · ● · · · · · · · · ·

In an effort to explain some of the educational opportunities available in the Memphis area, the State Technical Institute of Memphis sent faculty members to local inner-city high schools to speak to students and school counselors. Often the faculty member would find that the students had given little or no thought to their future.

On one of these visits, after explaining the opportunities available in his area of technology, the speaker asked the students where they wanted to be five years from now. Expecting answers concerning their jobs and financial future, the speaker was surprised when one young lady raised her hand and said, "At home with a baby." Although this was not the answer he wanted to hear, he expressed his awareness to the class that girls near the end of their high school years often thought of marriage and a family. The young lady again raised her hand and asked of the speaker: "What does marriage have to do with it?" After getting this and a variety of other responses, it became apparent that the young lady was not talking about marriage and a family, but about a baby and a welfare check.

To the speaker's surprise, this line of thinking appeared to be perfectly acceptable to the other students and was no surprise to the teacher and counselor. There seemed to be no understanding of the personal, social, and financial consequences of this mind-set.

The speaker, realizing that his information about technology and the job market could in no way solve the problem, wished the students well, thanked the teacher for allowing him to speak, and departed.

The personal consequences of such thinking are heartbreaking. If this young girl's plan is carried out, she will have little or no marketable skills, live in poverty, and have the awesome responsibility of raising a child or children. What chance does she and the child/children have for any kind of normal life?

All too often out of pure despair, the single mother turns to drugs. Some of these drug-addicted mothers give birth to the horror of drug-addicted babies. You might think this is something that seldom happens, but don't be fooled; it happens every day in hospitals in the Mid-South. This is just one of many undesirable results of this kind of reasoning.

We now have a system that was designed to reduce poverty but has instead allowed poverty to increase at an alarming rate. The financial results of this system are becoming more apparent every day as the national debt approaches $20 trillion.

In America, we have government of the people, which means that the people get to elect the government. It also means that the people are responsible for the government's expenses and debt. Each citizen's share of today's debt is about $60,000, and it increases by the minute. To find out how much you owe the federal government, simply divide the debt by the population of the country. This means that a family of four is roughly $240,000 in debt in addition to any personal debt such as housing, car, credit cards, and so forth.

Probably the biggest social evil of our welfare system is that it feeds upon itself. The children produced by this system often know of no other way to survive, and so generation after generation the problem grows.

I do not believe the federal government intended for the system to be used in this manner; however, it has made such irresponsible planning possible and has produced an entire culture that depends on the government for its survival. As this system continues to grow, feeding exponentially upon itself, the government has to borrow more and more money to support it. Nobody, not even the federal government, can continue to borrow more and more money indefinitely.

· · · · · · · ● · · · · · · · · ·

Last January, the Adverse Childhood Experience (ACE) Task Force released the results of a study that showed 55 percent of Memphis area adults had experienced traumatic events during their childhood—from abuse, neglect, and substance abuse to violence in the home. This is a staggering number, and it spans every race and socioeconomic group.

Recently, staffers with PBS *NewsHour* were in Memphis to film a show on the ACE Task Force, which focuses on attacking conditions that adversely affect early childhood development.

*NewsHour* will focus on the history of Memphis and how that history relates to adverse early childhood experiences, and how the city has overcome traumatic events such as floods, the yellow fever epidemic, and the assassination of Dr. Martin Luther King Jr. It is an ideal opportunity for Memphis, despite its reputation for crime, to be portrayed in a positive light about how the city is dealing with the prolific problem of crime and violence.

Crime and safety is the No. 1 concern on the minds of Memphis citizens, and people want immediate solutions—catch and imprison the criminals, which is understandable. However, for every criminal arrested, convicted, and incarcerated, there will be others to take their place. That is why the ACE Task Force is trying to find ways to eliminate or improve the conditions resulting in children turning into criminals.

ACE has identified the common denominator that negatively impacts the development of children: unstable families—including young single motherhood, low education attainment, and domestic violence.

These are the conditions that produce prolific numbers of children growing up to become criminals or adults who cannot properly function in society. While millions of tax dollars are being spent to prevent crime, prosecute offenders, and confine them in prison cells, would it not be less expensive to spend millions of dollars for intervention?

According to the Memphis *Commercial Appeal*, Shelby County (greater Memphis area) teens lead the state with the highest number of school suspensions and dropouts, and the highest teen pregnancy rate among the ninety-five counties in the state. Shelby County teens lead the state by far in sexually transmitted diseases. One out of every three Shelby County children under age eighteen lives in poverty. Do we not see a common denominator here?

"In many Memphis communities, it is common to become sexually active at an early age, as young as ten years old, and not to make school a priority," said psychologist Sidney Ornduff, who oversees mental health services for Shelby County Juvenile Court.

Ornduff pointed to the evidence of recent court cases when she said few teens realize how their personal choices seriously jeopardize or put an end to their plans for the future.[26]

For example, in one instance, a sixteen-year-old single welfare mother charged with a gun crime already had two children and said the second was a planned pregnancy. A thirteen-year-old charged with a delinquent act said she has a twenty-six-year-old boyfriend her parents are not aware of because she is rarely home.

Some girls in detention have told Ornduff that their parents are aware of them being sexually active as early as age twelve or thirteen, but they don't have access to birth control methods. Many of these young girls were themselves born to teen mothers.

Former Shelby County Juvenile Court Magistrate Claudia Halton said reducing the city's poverty and crime crisis begins with reducing teen pregnancies. Halton said she still remembers one of her last cases. A pregnant seventeen-year-old came into court and cried as she surrendered custody of the three children she already had and couldn't support.[27]

Memphis, with the highest rate of the state's African American population, had over one thousand babies born to girls ages fourteen to seventeen during the past year—more than the number in Tennessee's three other largest cities combined.

• • • • • • • • • ● • • • • • • • • • •

An African American friend and I were once having a friendly discussion about race. He said the only difference between us was the color of our skin. "We both want the same things," he said, "a good job, nice homes, good schools for our kids, and some disposable income." I agreed as I nodded my head to his description of the American dream. However, in many African American families, the American dream has been replaced by generational poverty—too many families that lack the necessary ingredients of parental support from two-parent families.

All too common is the story of a young black single mother whose real name is Princess. The name was given to her by a father she doesn't know. Princess doesn't live like royalty despite her name. She lives in a small government-subsidized apartment in North Memphis with her four-year-old-son, Travis. This is not the life Princess envisioned when she dropped out of school to have Travis. Princess was one of many teens whose moms grew up on welfare and maybe their grandmothers too. That's just the world they knew. Sadly, Princess and her son represent the future of too many young Memphis families.

Young single African American mothers living like Princess are now producing more babies in Memphis than any other group. They are having more babies than white moms, more than Hispanic moms, and more babies than African American moms who are married or who are living in stable middle-class households. Because of these realities, the next generation of poverty has already been born in the city.

Princess quit school in the ninth grade to have Travis. The father of her baby was in his twenties. "He kissed me and made me feel good, and was being my best friend,"[28] she said. She was asked why, at such a young age, she decided to sleep with an older man. "I didn't know any better. I didn't have anyone to tell me anything," Princess said. Princess's mother, who was a career welfare recipient, fought a losing battle with drugs and men her entire life. Princess has seven brothers and sisters, none of whom have the same father. Her mother, who died last year, didn't see Princess but once or twice in that last year. Princess, who grew up living with her grandmother, was recently asked to leave Grandma's house because there were too many other kids living there.

Princess has a stormy relationship with the father of her little boy. Court records show Princess has a restraining order against him, and she has been arrested for hitting him with a beer bottle. "He put his hand on me," she said, which is another way of saying she was beaten up.

With little education, no job, and a four-year-old son to raise, Princess gets $370 a month in food stamps and another $150 in direct payments, plus housing and several support vouchers because she has a baby. Princess and Travis's situation is not uncommon in Memphis.

Within the next five years, an estimated thirty-five thousand poor babies will be born in Memphis, or about the same number as the entire FedEx workforce here. The American Community Survey states that about twenty thousand babies were born in Memphis in 2015. African American mothers had about fourteen thousand of these babies. Of these, about seven thousand were born to mothers who are poor.[29]

Most of these young single moms will "get their own check and other government benefits," after having a baby, but it's not worth it. In the end, they will find themselves stuck in poverty and government dependence with nowhere to go.

An analysis by University of Memphis PhD demographer Elena Delavega reveals that in majority African American neighborhoods in Memphis, 85 percent of all children living there are born into poverty.[30]

Dr. Linda Moses, an African American obstetrician at the Regional Medical Center in Memphis, wonders what's going to happen to this city. Dr. Moses has delivered more babies to poor mothers than any doctor in the region.

The steadily increasing number of babies born to young single mothers covers a large part of Memphis and negatively affects schools, the criminal justice system, hospitals, and local government.

Not surprisingly, the neighborhoods with the most single mothers are also the areas with the highest proliferation of welfare recipients. They are the same neighborhoods that are the target of the Tennessee Achievement School District that oversees the worst performing five percent of all schools in Tennessee. For example, at Brookmeade Elementary School, one of the three elementary schools where Princess attended class, she received all Fs in most classes since 2010. Princess attended seven different schools before dropping out to have Travis. No one in Princess's family has ever graduated from high school.

The highest teen pregnancy rate in Memphis and the highest infant mortality rates in Memphis are in the zip code where Princess lives. The neighborhood where Princess rents an apartment has led the state in foreclosures for the last ten years. "It's not what I pictured," Princess said of her life. "It's a lot harder than I thought. I love Travis, but sometimes I wish someone had told me that having a child is a handful and takes away a lot of things you want to do as a teenager. But nobody told me any of that. I'm not saying that having a baby messed up my life, but it made it more complicated,"[31] said Princess.

Little Travis faces a rough road ahead because he was born into Memphis poverty. Travis has a very slim chance of graduating from college, according to research from the Brookings Institution. Quite the opposite is Brookings's analysis that shows a kid like Travis has a 30 percent chance of being in prison before he turns thirty, but only if he manages to graduate from high school. If he drops out before graduating from high school, his chances of going to prison before age thirty rises to 68 percent.

It only gets worse. As a child born into Memphis poverty to a single welfare mother, chances are good that Travis will live a chaotic childhood. His mother, after all, attended seven different schools before she dropped out to have him. The cycle of poverty that entraps children such as Travis can become permanent if there isn't early interference.

Princess's needs are great. The people in her life that she has counted on for emotional and financial support have let her down, starting with the absence of her mother and continuing with the father of her child. She needs some positive role models to provide guidance and emotional support. She plans to start working toward a GED diploma in January, a milestone for Princess since no one in her family has ever graduated from high school. Just before Christmas, Princess learned that her sister Tarieisha, age seventeen, is pregnant.

"A baby born to a poor, young single mother is twenty-five times more likely to remain in poverty his whole life compared to a kid born to a married couple and an older mom," said Ron Haskins, a highly respected poverty expert and codirector of the Center for Children and Families at Brookings. "The effect on kids' development from being poor and living in single-parent households is substantial. These kids are more likely to do poorly in school, more likely to drop out and more likely to commit a crime," said Haskins.

"Children learn through mimicking behavior by adults," said Cate Joyce, a researcher for the Urban Child Institute (TUCI). "We hope to reduce the number of children growing up in unstable, chaotic homes. Because, in a sense, that's the way the brain begins to wire itself." TUCI in Memphis reports that children born into poverty here often fall far behind in their social and cognitive skills by age three.

As a result of lagging behind in social and cognitive development, the vocabularies of kids growing up in unstable and chaotic homes may consist of no more than four hundred words by the time they start kindergarten. Also affected is their ability to get along with other kids. Many learn to fight early or to simply withdraw, which makes it harder for them to break out of poverty's hold.

We have thousands of kids like Travis growing up in Memphis right now, and, unless something changes, seven thousand more will be on the way next year and seven thousand more the year after that.

The overall poverty rate among African American households in Memphis has skyrocketed from 41.5 percent in 2007 to more than 60 percent in 2015, according to researcher Elena Delavega at the University of Memphis[32] Despite the myriad programs designed to help the poor, many are falling through the cracks, and that means trouble down the road.

Charlie Caswell, director of the Rangeline Neighborhood Community Center where Princess comes to pick up supplies to help take care of Travis, has seen these destructive characteristics over and over again. "Girls like Princess get around other young women who are all telling her the same story," Caswell said. "The girls are all saying that they are sleeping with dude because he's helping them pay bills," he predicted, "and there aren't many people in that environment who are saying to Princess that school is important." Until that culture is changed, we won't see much of a positive change in our community.

Not only is this lifestyle detrimental to the children and their families, but it places hardships on the rest of the population who pay the bills through higher taxes. And with taxpayers paying the bills, these actions continue, and we have an entitlement culture that has become a way of life. Until we change that norm, we won't see much of a change.

The Memphis *Commercial Appeal* ran a recent article entitled "19 years later, we still remember/Images of murdered mom remain with her children." The mother's name was Miriam Cannon, an African American single mother whose destructive life was a tragedy before she was murdered. Miriam was single, jobless, pregnant half of her life with five children under five years of age. If you read the newspaper every day, you will see the all-too-common scenario that has not changed much in nineteen years.

Hundreds of people and dozens of community and government programs are hard at work in Memphis in an attempt to change the city's culture of poverty. "Most teen mothers are single and many don't know what to do," Cate Price said. "Their own moms grew up poor and on welfare, and most of their grandmothers too. That's just the world they know."

With more than $5 billion in federal, state, and local assistance flowing into Memphis each year to fight poverty and help poor families, the poverty rate has only gone up, and it's been that way for decades. Some Memphis residents question why we (taxpayers) have allowed generations of people to grow up in this city completely void of responsibility?

How much longer can taxpayers expect to see the billions of dollars now coming into the city for poverty-related programs? There exist the issues of donor fatigue and poverty fatigue, where many well-meaning Memphians have simply decided the issues are too big, too impossible to solve.

With all the discussion about massive improvements in the Memphis area such as more sports centers in the inner city, Memphis continues to create debt as if money will solve the problems. None of these projects will eliminate or even make a dent in the problems of crime, poverty, and illiteracy. Memphis, like many large cities, can't buy its way to prosperity.

The businesses that have located here are usually promised tax breaks. In turn, the new businesses promise jobs to the Memphis area population, but the new or expanded businesses are unable to find a qualified workforce to fill the jobs.

In a recent article published by the Memphis *Commercial Appeal* newspaper in its Viewpoint Section, the city government is blamed for not doing something about the vicious cycle of poverty in the city. The problem is not with the city, but its 80 percent out-of-wedlock birth rate. Fourteen- to seventeen-year-old school girls giving birth to a child is the recipe for a "vicious cycle of poverty" that will never be broken, regardless of what the city might try to do.

Politicians should acknowledge the problem and take the lead in the battle of pregnancy prevention in teens and not ignore it as they do. If we continue to have teens and single mothers having the majority of babies, along with subsequent government dependency, the money to pay for new projects and lure new businesses will be depleted. With them go the tax base and jobs that are desperately needed.

Pregnancy prevention education needs to be taught with all the realities that actually occur in life. Whether it is abstinence or birth control, everyone, rich or poor, needs to be a warrior in this battle. The problems affect all of us.

If only the city's African American ministers would channel some of their enormous passion and energy toward teaching people how to be better parents, learn to settle disputes without violence, accept government assistance as a helping hand through tough times and not as a way of life, encourage children to get a proper education, discourage teenage pregnancies, and stop men from being just sperm donors in family situations, I believe the impact would be enormous in the black community, with "racism" being a thing of the past.

Much has been publicized about Memphis's failing schools. According to published salaries of Memphis school administrators, it appears we have some highly paid leaders in charge of our schools who, no doubt, work hard to educate our youth. But how many highly paid experts does it take to determine that poor parenting is usually the primary cause of poor students' lack of achievement? And that these disruptive kids steal the opportunity for a good education from other students who are there to learn and excel?

Once during the 2016 school year, parents of over one hundred Shelby County inner-city school students who were habitually absent from school were notified and asked to attend a meeting with the Shelby County district attorney. The parents were not going to be arrested, even though they all had warrants for their arrest for not sending their kids to school.

As stated in the notification, the DA's office wanted to work with these parents to get their kids in school and get them out of legal trouble. Of the more than one hundred parents notified, only six out of 117 showed up. Please, parents, you can do better. How do you expect your children to be better if you won't show up for something as important as getting an education? Get your kids to school—make your kids go to school. Take an interest in your child's life. Encourage him or her to complete his or her education and become a part of a "can-do" society versus a "what can you do for me" society. Do it not because you have to, but because you get to.

According to a recent editorial in the Memphis *Commercial Appeal*, "the spiking violent crime rate in Memphis is creating more chaos in troubled inner-city neighborhoods that are already rife with crime and the issues that feed it—poverty, single motherhood, blight, joblessness and low education attainment exacerbated by too many failing schools. Unless the city can find a way to solve these issues, crime will continue to be a problem."

Among the choices one makes that can place her in a life of perpetual poverty are the lack of education and the choice to become an unwed mother. However, it is important to realize that not all pregnancies are by choice—not all pregnancies are intentional. Many young girls become pregnant due to a lack of knowledge. A new government study suggests a lot of teenage girls have no idea of their chances of getting pregnant. Among thousands of teenage mothers who had unintended pregnancies, about a third said they didn't use birth control because they didn't think they could get pregnant.

Tragically, the number of local births to teenagers whose pregnancy is the result of rape is staggering. One case involved a twelve-year-old Memphis girl who ran away from home with her young baby. The baby was the result of her being raped over a two-year period by a then thirty-one-year-old man. This all too common occurrence is the worst of the worst, where the innocent child is forever damaged. Even sadder are the crime statistics that show the majority of rape cases to young children and teens are never reported.

· · · · · · ●●● ● ●●●●· · · · · ·

National statistics show that a mother who drops out of high school and has a baby without being married is a recipe for disaster, not to mention having multiple children with multiple fathers with whom she has no marital status or means of support.

Should we not ask ourselves who is most responsible, the young mother or a government whose liberal policies promote and encourage these behaviors? I remain amazed at how one of the primary causes of such a high poverty rate, which contributes to an out of control crime rate, is completely disregarded in Memphis.

If young girls are having babies one after the other, and living in the same household with other family members who are also having babies one after the other, and their primary source of income is "government benefits," is it any wonder that poverty rates increase in proportion to all the babies being born to teenagers or unmarried women?

Teens and other unmarried women who become pregnant were, in many cases, born to teen mothers themselves, and the intergenerational cycle must be broken. This behavior has persisted for decades, and, because of it, new generations will continue to perpetuate the cycle of living on taxpayers' dollars instead of working, and the poverty rate will never be reduced.

Claudia Halton is president and CEO of A Step Ahead Foundation. A Step Ahead, whose funding comes from sources in Memphis, is finding ways to get free long-term yet reversible birth control into the lives of all women.

Halton is a former juvenile court Judge and mother of grown children. She is a white woman in one of the poorest majority African American cities in America. Her former job involved determining whether young, single women with children were fit to be mothers or whether their kids needed to be taken away and put into foster care.

Halton describes one case as being heartbreaking. "A seventeen-year-old girl was standing there in front of me. She had three kids. I asked her 'Who is taking care of the kids?' She couldn't answer, and she was pregnant again."

Too many girls and young women in greater Memphis are getting pregnant with no means to support their kids. These young mothers want to make something of their lives. But once they have a kid too early, it's hard, if not impossible, for most of them ever to get ahead.

The purpose of A Step Ahead is this: to assist young women who don't have the money, are not knowledgeable about where to obtain contraception, and need help completing paperwork and other red tape associated with getting birth control. A Step Ahead works in conjunction with the Memphis Health Center and with six Christ Community Health Clinics in Memphis. These clinics have four types of reversible birth control devices on hand and will discuss them with anyone who visits one of the clinics. A Step Ahead reimburses the clinics for the total cost of the women's counseling and treatment. The foundation also staffs a hot line 24/7 so women can call any time day or night to get information. If necessary, the foundation even pays for transportation to and from the clinics.

Approximately fifty women a month have taken advantage of services from A Step Ahead providers. "What I know is that women really want to be able to control their lives, plan their futures, and get a step ahead," says Halton.

In addition to A Step Ahead, district attorneys across Tennessee have launched a campaign against teenage pregnancy. The "What's the Rush?" campaign is designed to inform young boys and girls about the legal, financial, and social consequences of becoming teenage parents.

The campaign, citing statistics from the National Campaign to Prevent Teen and Unwanted Pregnancy, emphasizes negative effects of teenage pregnancy including:

- Eight of ten teenage fathers do not marry the mother of their first child.
- Fewer than half of mothers who have a child before they are eighteen graduate from high school, and fewer than 2 percent have a college degree by age thirty.
- Teenage fathers have less education and earn much less money than teenage boys without children.
- The children of teenage mothers are more likely to be born prematurely and at a low birth weight, which can cause numerous health problems.
- Children of teenage mothers are 50 percent more likely to have to repeat a grade in school and are less likely to finish high school.
- The sons of teenage mothers are 30 percent more likely to end up in prison.

According to a recent report from the Centers for Disease Control, 66 percent of our high school students are sexually active. Should we not share some responsibility for educating them on how to avoid an unintended pregnancy when the consequences affect all of us? While abstinence is the first step, knowledge of other birth control options should be taught to our teens.

That being said, as a city and a community, we owe it to our children to teach them the negative facts of having a baby while they are still immature teenagers. Poverty is frequently the result of young parents having babies before they are able to finish school and begin careers. Family dysfunction and the drama that results when young moms and dads are children themselves are practically guaranteed.

If a teenage girl has a baby before graduating from high school, she will likely be one of the less than 60 percent who will go on to graduate. Only 48 percent of teen moms with more than one child will graduate or have a GED by twenty-two years of age. Poverty is almost a sure thing.

We should all be warriors in the battle against teen pregnancy. We need to use every available resource in our community to lower the teen pregnancy rate in Memphis, which is among the nation's highest. We all want our children to become independent adults, choose their own circumstances, and not let their circumstances determine the kind of life they and their future children and grandchildren will have.

The ultimate goal should be to teach teenagers not to have children while they too are children. This can be done by:

- Teaching abstinence.
- Teaching that sex without contraception leads to pregnancies and venereal disease, some cases of which last the rest of their lives.
- Teaching them that in all likelihood, teenage pregnancy will result in lives of poverty for those new, unprepared parents.
- Teaching them that having two-parent families, which many don't have, will make them more likely to have a prosperous life.

- Teaching what the different choices are for contraception to avoid unwanted babies.
- Teaching them that if you don't get pregnant you won't even think of needing an abortion for an unwanted child.

· · · · · · · ● · · · · · · · · ·

Availability of a skilled workforce is one of the determining factors that business and industry look for when determining where to locate or expand. Deborah Hester-Harrison, executive director of the Workforce Investment Network (WIN), a federally funded workforce development program, says she is aware of the lack of a skilled workforce in the Memphis and Shelby County area.

Deborah says "My time with WIN was a wake-up call on the state of the city's workforce and the volume of people who came through our career centers lacking the education and skills to get a decent job. We spend countless hours attempting to help these individuals, many of whom are single moms with two or three babies, less than a high school education and no job skills."[33]

It is important that we, as a community, realize that teen pregnancy is not just a reproductive issue. Teen pregnancy negatively affects profits of local businesses and makes attracting new businesses to the area difficult.

According to the Robin Hood Foundation, getting a high school diploma has been proven time and again as the single greatest factor between a life in poverty and a life of opportunity.

It is heartbreaking when seeing so many young people in this city drop out of school before graduating, knowing, in all probability, that their future holds low-skill jobs, limited opportunity to better themselves, welfare dependency, gang involvement, violence, incarceration, and early death for all too many.

These young people need all the hope and encouragement they can get before they make the decision to leave school. I would encourage more churches and businesses to participate in the "Adopt-A-School" program, where concerned citizens can interact with students and teachers and get to know them and their needs. Even reading to a class shows that you care.

We can help many of these failing students by becoming involved in their schools or community centers.

Despite the $5 billion in federal, state, and local funding flowing into Memphis each year with the purpose of fighting poverty and helping poor families, Shelby County leads the state in school dropout rates, pregnancy, poverty, and sexually transmitted disease. One could add crime to that list.

The answer to this crisis will never be more tax money and more police. A local psychologist said we must reverse the mind-set where it is "the thing to do," to become sexually active at an early age and not make school a priority. Many of these teens eventually become adults on the dole and in our correctional system.

As the Urban Child Institute has pointed out, teen mothers face daunting challenges. The majority are too immature to be responsible parents. Teen mothers usually lack the means to be self sufficient through education, job skills, and family role models. In Shelby County, many pregnant teens are unlikely to seek prenatal care. The absence of which has resulted in many babies born with low birth weights, which is primarily responsible for an excessively high infant mortality rate.

The National Campaign to Prevent Teen and Unplanned Pregnancy says, "Compared to those who delay childbearing, teen mothers are more likely to drop out of school, remain unmarried, and live in poverty. Their children are more likely to grow up poor, live in single-parent households; experience abuse and neglect, and enter the child welfare system."

According to the campaign's research, such early negative experiences can affect how the brains of young children grow. A child's brain is more vulnerable to trauma in the first three years of life than it is in later years. There were obvious differences in brain structure in children who were exposed to chaotic home life and insensitive parenting in their first years compared with children whose parents were more nurturing.

Many agencies in Memphis and Shelby County are dedicated to addressing the issue of teen pregnancy after the baby's birth, but prevention is what is needed most. It is a known fact that it costs less to prevent failure than to try to correct it later.

The answer to the problem is changing the "social norm." Poverty is not the cause; it is the result. In the 1930s and 1940s, when there was real poverty in both the white and black population, these problems were only a fraction of today's problems. Most households, regardless of race, had both parents and stressed individual responsibility, education, and faith as their first priorities.

Change starts in the home. Many of the problems in communities today are the result of poor choices based on the absence of a moral standard that pastors, parents, and community leaders could address and encourage. In our city where many black youths have become victims of crime and violence, most have not seized upon the importance of hard work or the power of education. Why? The first thing that comes to mind is the lack of parental guidance.

Black youths in this community deal with pressures that in my day were the exception, not the rule: raising a baby when you are practically a baby yourself, absence of a father in the home, lack of a good education, and no jobs for our youth. Tragically, what so many do have are the streets, and that's part of the problem.

Love, affection, hormones: put it all together, and bells start ringing, babies come along, all part of the intimacy package. We don't want to talk about it, but the cost of not having honest conversations about sex runs into the billions of dollars. When six out of ten babies in the African American community in Memphis are born to unwed mothers, the cost to the children and the government (taxpayers) is enormous.

Maybe these results speak more to religious beliefs than to political issues. But conservatives can, and should, realize the value of talking honestly about the costs and other negative results of unwanted pregnancies and sexually transmitted diseases. In the past ten years, both the teen pregnancy rate and the abortion numbers began to rise again after falling in the 1990s. These changes happened about the same time as the shift to abstinence-only education and a doubling of federal money spent on such programs.

Memphis and Shelby County are not alone when it comes to teen pregnancy. Adjacent to the southern border of Memphis is Mississippi, which, according to the Centers for Disease Control, has the highest teen birth rate in the nation: sixty-six per thousand teenagers, Arkansas, sixty-two, is No. 4 and Tennessee, fifty-six, is No. 8. The national average is forty-two.[34]

The Delta could be a poster child for proof that government dependency does not lead to prosperity. If trillions of tax dollars could solve problems, the Delta would be very wealthy indeed.

Former Mississippi Governor Haley Barbour, reflecting on his two terms as governor, stated that the No.1 problem in Mississippi is illegitimacy.

In this day and time, illegitimacy is a term that is seldom used because it stigmatizes a child born out of wedlock. But regardless of whether it is called "illegitimacy" or "teen pregnancy," the former governor was right by connecting the issue to many of the state's social ills. "Nothing else is close,"[35] Barbour says.

Barbour said that "an astonishing 55 percent of the children born in Mississippi last year were born to single mothers. Some of these kids will have both parents involved in raising the children, but the vast majority won't. They will be brought up by single mothers who will need government assistance or will work in low-paying jobs."

As Barbour pointed out, these mothers and their babies face a rough future. The children are six times more likely to be raised in poverty. They are more likely to drop out of school and depend on government assistance for their basic needs and health care. The children, most of all, will suffer the consequences—many, after dropping out of school, will end up in prison, costing all of us financially and as a society.

Not all children that are raised by single mothers or grow up poor fit this category. There are many examples where children raised in this type of environment have become successful, but the majority won't.

Barbour says,[36] "We've seen the dehumanizing effects of out-of-wedlock births in Mississippi and Memphis where the rate is about 80 percent and medical issues and crime are a continuous drag on efforts to make Mississippi and Memphis a state and city of choice."

Barbour pointed out in his interview that too many parents are not having heart-to-heart talks with their teenage boys and girls about sex and the dire consequences of having a child out of wedlock. Parents are not giving the issue enough attention, especially when high levels of hormones in teen bodies are saying yes!

That is why comprehensive sex education in schools is important. Some parents, lawmakers, and educators can hide their heads in the sand about the teen pregnancy problem. But it's not going away.

The United States has the highest rate of teen pregnancy among industrialized nations in the world. It is twice as high as the rate in Europe and the United Kingdom, and nearly ten times higher than the teen birthrate in Switzerland.

Teens need to know the negative facts about pregnancy and giving birth before marriage! Be a teenager and have a baby, and you will be poor—probably for the rest of your life. All of us are poorer and suffer socially because of the proliferation of poor, illiterate children that grow up without acquiring the skills to earn a decent living and that populate the Memphis Metropolitan area. But those that need this information the most are unlikely to read the newspaper or be exposed to those who could make a difference in their lives in a positive way.

Society needs to do several things. Show teenagers there are decent jobs available if they get an education, and keep emphasizing to them that if they have a baby as a teenager, in all probability they will be poor. Get other young single mothers to tell these girls that although the baby may be cute, in reality, their lives will not be their own due to taking care of the baby. There will be no money because most of the fathers do not contribute financially, and they will have a very limited social life because there is no money or time, and getting an education will be tough if not impossible.

We need to tell them how easy it is to get pregnant and how to avoid this. Abstinence is good, but a mother who teaches abstinence-only sex education to her daughter is called grandma. Birth control pills, diaphragms, condoms, and implants all can significantly reduce the likelihood of pregnancy.

Those who think informing their children of these facts will encourage them to have sex are mistaken. The more knowledge they have, the less likely they are to feel powerless and victims to their peers.

The secret to a productive life, above the poverty line, is quite simple: graduate from high school; don't have babies until you are married, and wait until you are at least twenty-one to start a family.

Until we attack the problem of unwed motherhood, we will make little progress on the issues of poverty, crime, and education in our city. Until we can change the culture of unwed mothers producing large numbers of illegitimate children, we will not be able to put an end to this ongoing problem.

Children cannot be expected to lead productive lives when from birth they are given minimal love, attention, and discipline from a family unit. Starting with a stable home life, values and morals need to be instilled early on by positive influences in their everyday lives.

Sex education should not be optional for teenage girls and boys. It should be taught along with basic core classes that every teen is required to take. In late 2012, legislators and Shelby County school officials convinced themselves that the best way to deal with teen pregnancy in Memphis is not to talk about it.

In Memphis, we have more than fifty nonprofit organizations working 24/7 to help serve the poor and unite our city. We have more than one thousand churches with outreach programs to serve and unite our city. We have thousands and thousands of people who volunteer their time, energy, and resources to help serve and unite our city. And don't forget the 99 percent of us who also make news—good news.

· · · · · · · ● ● ● ● ● ● ● ● · · · · · ·

*Chapter 3*

# DEFINITION OF POOR

I learned to give, not because I have much, but
because I know exactly how it feels to have nothing.

As an adult, I looked forward to visiting my parents in
Eastern Arkansas, but I dreaded the time spent in the
dated house. The only running water was in the kitchen.
With no operable hot water tank, the water was always ice
cold. In later years, portable window air conditioners were
installed, but Daddy, who was reluctant to accept modern
conveniences, didn't like to run them, so we suffered in
the heat.

Other definitions of poverty are the big-city areas
where postal workers fear for their lives when delivering
mail, and where shootings, murders, and robberies occur
on a daily basis. Where house after house in inner-city
neighborhoods have bars on every window and door.

Poverty robs people of their dreams. It is the underlying
force that keeps pulling families down. If we allow it
to consume us, it creates dependence, hopelessness, and

diminishing revenue for Mid-South businesses, as well as prematurely lost lives through crime and violence. The statistical data is clear. Memphis poverty is the nation's highest in many categories. Memphis is the center of the Mid-South, and poverty is a consuming problem that impacts our entire Mid-South area.

According to the Population Reference Bureau, approximately 80 percent of people in this poverty group have Social Security as their only means of retirement income. Eighty percent in this group do not have life or health insurance. Ninety-three percent do not have a savings account, and 95 percent do not have a will.

I've wondered how many of the economically challenged have thought of what would happen to them if the government should go broke and fail to deliver on the promise of continued support?

Family breakdown or lack of a father figure in the home has been proven to contribute to poverty, low test scores in poor performing schools, drug use, violent crime, and sexual promiscuity. Liberal politicians like to claim that racism is primarily responsible for problems of the poor, but in reality, excessive government dependency creates generational poverty.

Out-of-wedlock births have escalated to 30 percent nationally—70 percent among African Americans, according to the Census Bureau and the US Department of Health and Human Services. Also shown is that seven out of ten youths in the criminal justice system came from single-parent homes.

Walter E. Williams is an African American professor of economics at George Mason University who recently wrote a syndicated column on poverty. He quoted a statement made by liberal academics and lawmakers: "People were not just struggling because of their personal deficiencies. There were structural factors at play. People weren't poor because they made bad decisions. They were poor because our society creates poverty." Williams states, "To say our society creates poverty is breathtakingly ignorant."

According to our American history books, the United States, in 1776, was among the poorest nations in the world, but in less than two centuries we became the world's richest nation. Americans who today are considered poor have more material goods than middle-class people did as recently as the 1960s.

Dr. Robert Rector and Rachel Sheffield give us this information: "Eighty percent of poor households have air conditioning. Nearly three-fourths have a car or truck, and 31 percent have two or more. Two-thirds have cable or satellite TV. Half have one or more computers. Forty-two percent own their own homes. The average poor American has more living space than the typical nonpoor person in Sweden, France, or the UK. Ninety-six percent of poor parents said their children were never hungry during the year because they couldn't afford food. There is no comparison between the median standard of living today and that in earlier periods."[37]

Dr. Williams goes on to say, "The poverty rate among blacks is 36 percent. Most black poverty is found in female-headed households, but the poverty rate among black married couples has been in single digits since 1994 and stands today at seven percent. Today's black illegitimacy rate is 72 percent, but in the 1940's, it was around 14 percent."[38]

Dr. Williams asked these questions: "Is having babies without the benefit of marriage a bad decision, and is doing so likely to affect income? Are dropping out of school and participating in criminal activity bad decisions, and are they likely to have an effect on income? Do people have free will and the capacity to make decisions, or is their behavior a result of instincts over which they have no control?"[39]

As a black person, Dr. Williams says he is glad the message taught to so many of today's black youths wasn't taught in the 1930s, '40s, and '50s when the civil rights struggle was beginning. He said the admonishment he frequently heard from black adults back then was, "Be a credit to your race."[40]

Many politicians believe the federal government should take care of the poor through subsidies and entitlements with no thought that the poor person is at all to blame or responsible for his or her situation, which is often repeated from one generation to the next.

Unfortunately, most of the economically challenged put too much trust in their elected officials and church ministers, who are often highly influenced by liberal politicians. I cannot help but wonder why pastors in African American churches do not do more to discourage out-of-wedlock births, which in turn perpetuate government dependency, resulting in poverty and crime.

In Memphis, the role of the church in its outreach missions, especially in the African American community can't be overstated. Just 21 percent of black children in Memphis are being raised in a "husband-wife family," according to data from the 2010 Census, compared with 68 percent of white children. Churches have the means and ability to change this culture. They can influence the mind-set among their congregation and in their neighborhoods if they dedicate themselves to the task.

Today, with far too many African American young people killed through black-on-black crime, the problem of poor parenting is all too clear in every aspect of life. In Memphis, the school system struggles with issues of poverty and learning disabilities. The job market needs skilled and committed workers, but the work ethic of the hip-hop generation is at an all-time low. We have too many teenage mothers, and the nation's prisons are overrun with young people making bad choices.[41]

A major factor contributing to these dire conditions is the absence of fathers in the lives of their children. We repeatedly observe young girls gravitating toward older men for the missing affections of a father and winding up pregnant. Young teenage boys are lured into gang membership looking for that father figure. Searching for missing love and affection, they often become premature parents caught up in the welfare framework, or worse, the criminal justice system.

Crime is a symptom and not the root problem. The world of crime is filled with brilliant young minds that simply made some bad choices, and society has not gone far enough in providing a second chance. On the flip side, a large percentage of felons, both black and white, are illiterate, with below average IQs. Felons are perpetually punished, and the labels and stigma given young mothers only marginalizes another generation for mediocrity.

The role of education is clear. Some of the resources in place to target higher-risk groups in the Memphis area are: Team Read, math and reading labs, resource classes, and special tutoring. Higher-risk children must be embraced, not walled off in isolated pockets of poverty. Better decisions simply can be expected among children who are shown that they cannot only succeed but that they can play important roles in the community. Better decisions will lead to fewer teenage pregnancies, a higher level of achievement in school, and a deeper sense of responsibility.

For various reasons, a cycle of unplanned pregnancies, unwanted children, and an increasing number of one-parent families, most of them headed by women with no husband present, has taken hold in Memphis and is being repeated through multiple generations. It doesn't have to be that way.

The government's answer to this is to put more money into job training programs, additional benefits, and so forth. The tragedy is that when government programs replace common sense, the careless poor are destined to a life of perpetual poverty. Some politicians believe they are doing the poor a favor by addicting them to a government subsidized life when, in reality, the result may be the catastrophic loss of a generation of people.

Unfortunately, many in the poor population have bought into untruths perpetuated by social media and the left that say poor people are poor because rich people are rich. In reality, 60 percent of American kids are growing up in homes with no father. In Memphis and other large cities with a high African American population, the figure is in excess of 80 percent.

According to the National Center for Children in Poverty, if Mississippi high school graduates don't go on to college, there is a 77 percent chance that their children will grow up in poverty—well above the 67 percent national average.

The Department of Health and Human Services reports that over three million children are abused each year, a number that is no doubt conservative. Many of them have been the victims of domestic violence, rape, or incest. Children abused and killed while in the care of the mother's boyfriend is an all too common occurrence in the Memphis area.

Take the case of Shamia Ivory, an eighteen-month old girl who was beaten to death by her mother's boyfriend. The mother, Shamira Ivory, testified in court that she did not immediately call 911 because she thought her listless daughter only had a stomachache. Shamira said she went out for cigarettes, and when she returned about fifteen minutes later, her boyfriend, Gary Hawkins, told her the baby threw up. Ivory claimed she cleaned her daughter up but was not worried even though the baby was lifeless. When the prosecutor handed her a picture of the child's body showing her stomach covered with bruises, she asked the mother if it didn't look like somebody beat the stew out of her.

Despite Shamira's attempts to cover for Hawkins, he was convicted and sentenced to prison. Shamira, a single mother on welfare, has six other children, including one born in jail several months after her daughter was killed.[42]

A Memphis woman was recently arrested after police found her three children unattended in a car while she had her nails done. In the car, along with the three children, police reported finding a loaded handgun, but not before the woman's two-year-old son picked it up and pointed it at officers.

After a concerned citizen notified police, they reported finding the three children—ages four, two, and nine months—inside a car in the parking lot. As they approached the car, the woman came out of the salon and told the officers the children were hers and that she had just stepped inside to use the bathroom. However, according to a police affidavit, officers checked the salon's appointment log and found the woman had spent the previous hour or so getting a full-set nail service. The woman was held after she could not produce a driver's license. Erika Williams, a single welfare mother, was charged with unlawful possession of a weapon, marijuana possession, and three counts of leaving her children unattended in a motor vehicle.

Here in the Deep South, poverty cycles from generation to generation like in no other area of the nation. Time-worn problems of premature single parenthood and limited education dim the chances of having a middle-class life for somebody born into generational poverty.

How do we convince not only welfare recipients but our liberal population that the answer to having a successful life free from government dependency is personal responsibility—not the welfare system! Personal responsibility means—among other things—getting an education, developing a good work ethic, and delaying having children until you can afford to take care of them. Opportunities to leave welfare and poverty behind are attainable!

What keeps the poor population in the status quo? Most put too much trust in the word of elected officials. They hand over their children for the government to educate and their freedom in exchange for government-mandated rent control and other benefits.

If a terrorist can change someone's mind and convince him or her to become a suicide bomber, we can surely change the mind-set of young people for the good and convince them that education and personal responsibility is the way to bring about humanity, peace, and a better life.

*Chapter 4*

# RACISM

Looking around at our world it is time to rebuild
new bridges and reach out to each other with a love
that can no longer be ignored or abandoned.
                                    —Maya Angelou

Many of today's leaders like to blame social ills on racism.
Intentionally or not, these leftist leaders have encouraged
too many African Americans to depend on the federal
government for their livelihood. Politicians want social
programs kept in the hands of the government regardless
of their ineffectiveness. Time and again, statistics have
proven the two are intertwined, not by race but by culture.

Talk-show host and author Bill O'Reilly recently
delivered an impassioned message on the subject of the
race problem facing America and the lack of leadership
by the president to solve those issues. O'Reilly blamed the
disintegration of the family, the entertainment industry,
and drug dealers.

O'Reilly surmised that many young black men raised without structure reject education and gravitate toward drugs, hustling, and gangs. Quoting O'Reilly: "The reason there is so much violence and chaos in the black precincts is the disintegration of the African American family. That drives poverty, and the lack of involved fathers leads to young boys growing up resentful and unsupervised. Raised without much structure, young black men often reject the education process and gravitate towards vice."[43]

A major finding of a new report issued by the Urban Institute, a liberal think tank, found that many of the same social issues highlighted in a landmark 1965 study on black family structure have worsened over the last fifty years.[44] The institute reexamined the circumstances of black families nearly five decades after Senator Patrick Moynihan wrote his controversial report on the breakdown of the traditional family as the main cause of problems in the black community. He was concerned that while black unemployment was decreasing, the number of blacks on welfare was increasing.

The Moynihan report looked at social disparities between white and black families and the need for government intervention. It focused on high unemployment rates, crime, poverty, unwed parenting, and other social ills that pushed many black families into a continuing cycle of dysfunctional long-term poverty.

Since Moynihan issued the report in 1965, things have worsened. At that time, one out of every four black babies was born to unmarried women. Over the next fifty years, the number of black children born to unmarried women had tripled.

The report's position was that the rise of female-headed black households diminished the authority of black men, leaving them unable to serve as responsible fathers and providers. The report suggested the breakdown of the black family was primarily responsible for poverty and an increase in welfare. Many black leaders criticized the report at the time, saying it was filled with stereotypes and played down the effects of discrimination and racism.

Gregory Acs, director of the Urban Institute's Income and Benefits Policy Center, says in Moynihan's report that his main conclusion about the importance of traditional families has been vindicated by research that shows children from two-parent families fare better educationally, financially, and emotionally than those from single-parent homes.[45]

Nationally, 70 percent of African American children are born out of wedlock and wind up living with a single mother or some other family member. Many times the father shows no interest in providing for the baby's welfare or upbringing. Without a father figure to instill discipline and structure in the home, the children, many times, learn social values on the street.[46]

If parents fail to show their youngsters the benefits of getting an education as a means of bettering themselves, they become excellent targets for gangs, drugs, and violence. According to the Memphis *Commercial Appeal*, the high school dropout rate in Memphis is at 50 percent, many of these being second-generation dropouts.

Why, then, would any private small-business owner, or a successful industry, want to hire someone who didn't have at least a high school education that would enable that person to demonstrate that he or she already had a skill learned in class or had the ability to learn a skill on the job? One of the core problems of this situation is, sadly, the gradual demise of the African American family unit.

But this situation won't be discussed by the liberal left, which would rather convince African Americans that they are victims. I feel sorry for people who are easily manipulated to believe this and don't do their own research.

Black people in Memphis can look with pride that we have had an African American president, a black mayor, black police chief, and many prominent personalities on all local TV channels, and see the advantages of a proper education.

In a debate over racism with a highly influential African American minister, Star Parker relates this experience in her book *Uncle Sam's Plantation.*

> Men and women like this minister and his willing accomplices in the liberal establishment are involved in the slave trade, as surely as if they had put chains on the people themselves. They work in ghettos instead of the fields, dutifully putting their master back in the Senate or House of Representatives so they'll

keep those compassionate benefits coming. They get power, we get a free ride. Everybody wins. Except we don't. The results have been disastrous.

I know the social problems affecting the black Americans are great. I know that confronting black anger is exhausting. But I also know the dream of my ancestors did not include enslavement on the government's plantation of poverty. They understood that nothing in the world is greater than freedom, and I know from personal experience that freedom will never come from dependence on the welfare state.

· · · · · · · ●●● ● ●● · · · · · · ·

During the great Depression, when hard times were at their worst, communities pulled together, families and neighbors helping each other with little or no idea given to reliance on the federal government. This comparison, however, did not extend to black families. After the civil war, racial scorn and abuse of blacks spread rapidly.

African Americans experienced years of racial injustice after slavery ended. Even American religious communities turned a deaf ear on the harsh treatment of blacks. Jews, as survivors of the Holocaust, were at first sympathetic to the plight of American blacks. However, when black activists became increasingly political and vocal, Jews began to separate themselves from the movement. Jews did not look to the government to solve their social and economic problems. They wanted to take care of their own business.

Throughout the last fifty years, while blacks have focused on political redress for racism only to see neighborhoods and families fall apart, Jewish businesses thrived with successful family and community lives.

The reason for people from all over the world wanting to come to America was for opportunity. In its early days, people came to America seeking freedom. To them, freedom meant the opportunity to make a better life—a life without government intervention.

Racism is often blamed for the black communities' poverty, lack of education, crime, lack of job opportunities, etc. If that is the case, why doesn't the Asian community (for instance) have these problems?

How did other struggling communities of people start in similar situations and end up in totally different circumstances? Was it racism or lack of government dependency that made the difference?

Children of poor immigrants get an education and then in one generation move into middle-class America. Why, then, do a large percentage of black Americans remain poor? Racism? Don't think so. Poverty in black homes with married parents is well below the national average. The appalling rate of children born out of wedlock is now a systemic condition that sentences each new generation to another cycle of poverty.

*Chapter 5*

# GOVERNMENT BENEFITS

For thou shall eat the labor of thine hands; happy
shall thou be and it shall be well with thee.
—Psalm 128:2

In her book *Uncle Sam's Plantation*, African American Star
Parker relates her experience with the welfare system: "Let
me make sure I understand you correctly," she inquired
of the welfare case worker as she presented her with her
pregnancy confirmation note from a doctor. "All I have
to do for you to send me $465 a month, $176 worth of
food stamps, and 100 percent free medical and dental
assistance is to keep the baby. As long as I don't have a
bank account, find a job, or get married, I qualify for aid?
Where do I sign up?"

Star further states she desired designer clothes and
a lavish lifestyle, but she simply refused to work hard,
stating she blamed racism, her parents, and any other

excuse society would allow her to use. Sadly, Star states that her attitude and actions led her deeper into poverty. Just imagine this scenario repeated hundreds of thousands of times.

Why has welfare become a way of life in many of our inner cities? It is free. You are given free medical care, free day care, food stamps, housing assistance, transportation, and, for school children—free breakfast, lunch, after-school snacks, and free lunches during summer months.

The Heritage Foundation reports welfare spending in America amounts to more than $1.2 trillion every year That is more than a million tax dollars a day being spent on welfare programs.

We have women producing numerous offspring whether or not they have the capacity to take care of the children's basic life needs. Heartbreakingly, the legacy is our violent inner cities and the explosion of fatherless children.

Since authorization of The War on Poverty Act of 1965, and trillions of dollars later, poverty is the same, but African American families are not. With triple the number of single-parent homes, entitlements have all but relieved many black fathers of their parental responsibility and paved a road to lives of crime, filling the nation's prisons.

The 1960s Great Society began with a well-meaning government program that was supposed to lift the country's poor out of destitution. However, we went from social building to social control. Rather than taking care of issues of poor people, government welfare created the sort of issues that will unavoidably happen when individuals turn their lives over to the government.

When individuals discovered that having babies they couldn't afford ultimately carries bigger paychecks with each extra child, the scale of entitlements exploded, with negative results to the general public.

There is the case of Desmond Hatchett of Knoxville, Tennessee. Desmond doesn't deny fathering thirty children by eleven different women; instead he is pleading with the state of Tennessee to help him out with child support. Hatchett, just thirty-three, appeared in a Knoxville court to make his case.

Holding a minimum wage job, he already gives half his pay to the children. Because he has a minimum wage job, some of the eleven moms get just $1.49 a month in support. The children range in age from toddlers to fourteen. "I had four kids in the same year, twice," he said in explaining how he set the pattern.[47] Court officials noted that Hatchett had not broken any laws fathering so many children, and that the state had no means to require him to stop. Unfortunately, any mention of cutting back on government charity is considered racist and heartless.[48]

Years ago, the majority of the US media aligned themselves with the civil rights movement. However, most in the media did not fully understand the long-term negative effects caused by taking away the motivation to accomplish the American dream through pride of one's own accomplishments.

The new system, which grew into the Great Society, was lauded in liberal circles but, as a general rule, hurt poor people. Welfare explosion was the outcome, with entitlements helping poor people but making them more reliant on the federal government. This dependency has evolved into a lifestyle for a significant number of poor people, harming those they proposed to help and denying them the chance for self-sufficiency and a feeling of pride and self-accomplishment.

In the late 1960s, when President Lyndon Johnson declared the "War on Poverty," which came to be known as the "Great Society," the lion's share of black families in the United States lived in two-parent homes. By 2005, only one in five black homes had two-parent families.[49]

As the black family came apart, single-mother births resulting in a rise in crime, drug use, promiscuity, and sexually transmitted diseases, and school dropouts exploded. The black poverty rate has remained double the national average since the Great Society began despite trillions of dollars spent.

Doubtlessly, our leaders neglected to predict the staggering impact their policies would have on the self-esteem and pride of accomplishment of the black population. However, the real losers were the blacks themselves. Suffering from hopelessness and low self-esteem, African Americans were drawn into a false sense of complacency, not hard to do when demoralized people were convinced their only hope was government dependency.[50]

After fifty years of living under Great Society policies, there exists a poverty field in many of our inner cities that is run by the federal government, overseen by the liberal media, and paid for by our taxpaying citizens.

Dr. Martin Luther King's dream of the "promised land" was a superior world for individuals of all colors and races. However, in many cases, blacks have unknowingly moved in the opposite direction. Many would believe that the Great Society has negatively affected many black Americans and enslaved them in a fashion similar to slavery.

In fact, many individuals believe that if it had not been for the government protecting the slaveholders, slavery would not have remained the travesty it was in America for so long. President Lincoln issued the Emancipation Proclamation in 1863, yet beginning with the 1960s "Great Society," slavery, but in a more unobtrusive way, again raised its evil head. That is the point at which the federal government began its own plantation with the Office of Personnel Management (OPM) used to subjugate poor people.[51]

The Welfare Reform Act of 1996 combined Aid to Families with Dependent Children (AFDC), with the Job Opportunities and Basic Skills Program, and formed the Temporary Assistance for Needy Families (TANF) Program. This program gives money to offspring of families whose father or mother is missing, handicapped, deceased, or unemployed.

The Housing Assistance Program Act provides housing if the recipient's household income falls below 50 percent of median family income. This entitles the recipient to be placed on a waiting list for Section 8 Housing provided by OPM.

The Housing and Urban Development program, called HUD, provides rental assistance programs in inner city neighborhoods in the Memphis area. These government assistance programs are intended to provide safe low-cost housing for the poor and low income, while providing an opportunity for them to improve their lives. However, the majority of these apartment complexes have serious crime and maintenance problems. The face of public housing has changed from a place where families could live in a clean, safe environment until they could afford to own a home of their own to permanent communities of poverty and crime.

Since the late 1960s, these apartment communities do not resemble the original purpose of HUD's rental assistance program, which was to change people's lives toward more positive outcomes. "That cannot happen," states Robert Lipscomb, an African American and city director of Housing and Community Development, "if the people whose actions made public housing enclaves of poverty, crime and hopelessness, are unwilling to change."[52]

"I know that sounds harsh," says Jerome Wright, a black columnist for the Memphis *Commercial Appeal*, "but the reality is that actions of some families—not all— in the projects, contribute to the crime and dire housing conditions."[53]

Ruby Bright, executive director of the Women's Foundation for a Greater Memphis, says the foundation has launched a major poverty-reduction effort in the 38126 zip code, one of the poorest in Memphis. Bright says, "We want to walk with families, not carry them. You cannot help people who are not willing to help themselves. People have to take some responsibility for making their lives better, including taking advantage of programs that provide them with the support needed to make the change."[54]

Many of the families that occupy these apartments are caught up in a cycle of generational poverty, fueled by bad choices: children raising children, such as the single mother raising her ten children on public assistance whose picture appeared in one morning's *Commercial Appeal*. Tragically, her apartment caught fire, destroying most of the family's possessions. She and all her children escaped the fire, but help was badly needed to assist the family.

Food stamps are accessible for low-salaried families to maintain a healthy diet. The Women, Infants, and Children's Program (WIC) is part of the Child Nutrition Act of 1966, which provides food assistance for pregnant and postpartum women and their babies, as well as any other children up to five years of age. All TANF recipients receive free child care. Medicaid provides free health care for the needy, including prenatal care, child birth, and postnatal care.[55]

The Tennessee Department of Human Services (DHS) manages the Child and Adult Care Food Program and a summer food program for children. In operating the programs in Tennessee, DHS distributes close to $80 million in federal tax dollars each year to contractors providing snacks and meals to day-care centers, mobile lunch buses, and recreational programs. They feed 180,000 Tennessee children during the school year and forty-two thousand children each day during the summer months. This is only a few of the seventy-seven federal welfare programs paid for by our government. Is it any wonder that welfare is the most coveted lifeline of so many?[56]

At a cost in excess of $56 billion a year, the Earned Income Tax Credit (EITC), is the third-largest social welfare program in the United States, after Medicaid ($275 billion federal and $127 billion state funds), and food stamps ($78 billion). Almost thirty million American households received more than $56 billion in payments through EITC in 2015. These EITC dollars had a significant impact on the lives and communities of the nation's lowest-paid working people, largely repaying any payroll taxes they may have paid.

Enacted in 1975, the initially modest EITC has been expanded by tax legislation on a number of occasions, including the widely publicized Tax Reform Act of 1986, and was further expanded in 1990, 1993, 2001, and 2009. Today, the EITC is one of the largest antipoverty tools in the United States.[57]

Has the EITC changed the poverty rate in the United States? A resounding no, as the poverty rate has remained the same since the 1960s despite this and an overwhelming scale of other entitlements.

A more responsible national political leadership would enact policies that encourage personal responsibility and discourage self-destructive behavior by not subsidizing people who live irresponsibly. I would suggest phasing out government assistance in such instances. A more appropriate form of assistance could be provided by churches; charitable organizations, such as the Memphis Food Bank; and a myriad of other outreach programs that exist in the city. We have provided billions and now trillions of dollars in government entitlement programs for the last fifty years. Not only has poverty and crime worsened, but the end result has been our violent inner cities and the explosion of fatherless children.

I would also suggest phasing out government assistance after the birth of one or two dependent children rather than increasing assistance with larger paychecks after the birth of each additional child. For example, should anyone be allowed to be a parent of more out-of-wedlock children than they can support? Should there be negative consequences (i.e., removal of children from the home or encouraging birth control such as tubal ligation or other forms of birth control? Or should we continue to give welfare mothers larger checks for each additional child?

Should we maintain the status quo, or do we have the courage to properly address these issues? "What about the children?" I am sure to be asked. My passion *is* people—especially children. Because of my compassion for and love of children, I was once offered a four-year grant to study and major in early childhood services at a large hospital in Bethesda, Maryland. In offering the grant, the hospital administrator, who was a former neighbor, wrote that he and others in our church thought I had a special gift for working with children.

During my growing up years, when government benefits and welfare were nonexistent, neighbors helped each other through hard times. Orphanages existed for children whose parents could not care for them financially or otherwise. Neglected or abused children were placed in these homes either temporarily or permanently for their own safety. While certainly not the ideal home life as in a two-parent family, orphanages offered structure, a safe environment without crime and violence, and the likelihood of obtaining a high school diploma. With our country's foster care system leaving much to be desired, replacing foster care and the welfare system with orphanages may be expensive, but far from the $1.3 trillion currently spent on entitlements. Massive bloodshed and incarceration among young men and women could be a thing of the past.

I know this sounds idealistic and maybe unrealistic. But Memphis and the rest of our country have too much going for them to be dragged down by deadly violence and senseless mayhem.

It is unacceptable that because of our children's environment or station in life, they too often become the victims or perpetrators of crime. We know of them only through a mug shot or a memorial—a child we did not reach.

The current policy, no doubt, encourages rather than discourages this lifestyle. While this may seem a bit harsh to some, I contend what is truly harsh is continuing policies that encourage irresponsible behavior resulting in a culture that appears to be bent on destroying one another.

Until we address these issues, I believe all other efforts to control rampant violent crime are doomed to long-term failure. Until changes are made in the way our government (local, state and federal) condones negative lifestyles, and until it provides consequences for them, government benefits and all of the best education in the world will not make a difference.

In my generation, success was based on the idea that if a man worked hard, bought a piece of property, got married before having children, and saved a little along the way, he and his family would be successful.

Civil rights organizations headed by the Jesse Jacksons, Al Sharptons, and Louis Farakahns of the world search for prejudice behind nonminorities in organizations, schools and universities, clubs, churches, social gatherings, and police forces. These leaders could have a world-changing effect in the lives of African Americans if their leadership talents were used to encourage personal responsibility.

In the end, it becomes an empty joke. These leaders who work to keep the welfare framework the status quo are responsible for using their political clout to promote liberalism and socialism. They strive to manipulate and control the poor for power, prestige, political gain, and money. As long as our political climate remains the status quo, efforts to liberate the poor from a system of government reliance would only be eclipsed by the liberation of slaves by Abraham Lincoln.

What is viewed as "moral impoverishment" today compared to prior to the '60s, happened the same time the federal government began subsidizing individual irresponsibility by way of the Great Society. That's when society started in a big way to take care of people who made poor choices about (1) having children (Aid to Families with Dependent Children) and (2) being unemployable and "poor" by dropping out of school (food stamps and other welfare programs). Coincidence? Many would not think so.

There was a time when Americans would have been embarrassed to take, much less ask for, anything from their fellow citizens. If you were able-bodied, asking for help from the government was regarded by a previous generation as moral weakness. Take the case of my father, who was partially disabled as the result of an accident and refused to even discuss government help.

Welfare programs have done enormous damage in black America. Reliance on the government has created a situation in which out-of-wedlock birth rates, especially in the black community, have soared. This begs to ask if the government should get out of the social program business and let the religious community fill that void. It is not the government's place to reconcile people and encourage personal responsibility. It should be the role of churches to take the lead! In the words of former President Ronald Reagan, "Often the government is the problem, not the solution."

Washington, DC, has one of the highest rates of poverty in the nation. Its child poverty rate is the nation's worst. Its public school system, with a graduation rate of less than 50 percent, is the nation's worst.

Leftist leaders encourage government dependency at all cost. The result? Look at DC, Detroit, Chicago, Baltimore, Oakland, Milwaukee, St. Louis, and Memphis. The thing all these cities have in common, in addition to an extremely high homicide rate, is a large government-dependent population run by liberal politicians. Can we not see a common denominator here?

The liberal left wants to keep poor people dependent on the government; make them promises, and ensure their stay in office. They prefer this to helping small businesses and bringing companies back to America that would help furnish meaningful jobs. As Star Parker says, "Thanks to our billions of dollars in welfare aid, our rural plantations have been transferred to inner city plantations and are alive and well."

It should be distressing to all American citizens as we see our large inner cities turning into a modern-day Sodom. Wake up, America! Is modern culture really that out of touch with the needs of our children?

· · · · · · · ● ● ● ● ● · · · · · · · ·

In 1887, Alexander Tyler, a Scottish history professor at the University of Edinburgh, had this to say about the fall of the Athenian Republic some two thousand years prior:

> A democracy is always temporary
> in nature; it simply cannot exist as

a permanent form of government. A democracy will continue to exist up until the time that voters discover that they can vote themselves generous gifts from the public treasury. From that moment on, the majority always votes for the candidates who promise the most benefits from the public treasury, with the result that every democracy will finally collapse over loose fiscal policy, (which is) always followed by a dictatorship.

Tyler goes on to say:

The average age of the world's greatest civilizations from the beginning of history has been about 200 years. During those 200 years, these nations always progressed through the following sequence:

From bondage to spiritual faith;
From spiritual faith to great courage;
From courage to liberty;
From abundance to complacency;
From complacency to apathy;
From apathy to dependence;
From dependence back into bondage.

Professor Joseph Olson of Hamline University School of Law in St. Paul, Minnesota, states his belief that the United States is now somewhere between the "complacency and apathy" phase of Professor Tyler's definition of democracy, with some 40 percent of the nation's population already having reached the "governmental dependency" phase.

· · · · · · ●●● ●●● · · · · · · ·

Sadly, the black poverty rate has hardly changed since the late 1960s. Should this not raise eyebrows when during this same timeframe, thousands of immigrants from different nations around the world have come to America with very little and moved into the middle class in one generation with no government assistance?

Today, we are suffocating in a red ink of entitlements. Welfare and entitlement spending is out of control. Welfare spending alone in the United States now surpasses $1.2 trillion a year!

Legislators at both the state and federal levels talk in numbers that most folks can't grasp. So how much is a billion? What does it mean when we say something cost $1 billion in the United States? It is difficult to visualize just how many dollars there are in $1 billion. The politicians who are spending fortunes in government money make it sound as though they are dealing in smaller numbers by removing quite a few digits. For example, $500,000,000,000 is simply stated $500 billion. To put just $1 billion into perspective:

- If we wanted to pay down $1 billion of the US debt, paying one dollar a second, it would take thirty-one years, 259 days.

- About one billion minutes ago, the Roman Empire was existent and Jesus was alive. (One billion minutes is about nineteen hundred years.)
- About one billion hours ago, we were living in the Stone Age. (One billion hours is about 114,000 years).
- About one billion months ago, dinosaurs walked the earth.

Multiply any of the scenarios by five to see what welfare is costing taxpayers annually.

A trillion dollars is even more incomprehensible. A trillion is a thousand billion.

- One trillion seconds equals 1,688 years.
- The oldest known human was alive 110 trillion seconds ago.
- The US National Debt at the time of this writing is $20,000,000,000,000 or more simply stated: $20 trillion. The number is so large that the $1.75 billion this debt is increasing per day seems miniscule by comparison. If the national debt was paid off at a rate of $10 million a day, it would take five thousand years to repay, and it's going deeper every day.

So, the next time you hear a politician casually use the words "billion" or "trillion," think about whether you really want that politician spending your tax money.

· · · · · · · · · ● · · · · · · · · ·

Is it not time for another era of black Americans to come forward? Is it not time for a generation that will advocate for family values and personal responsibility? One that will lead black families and black communities back to the mountaintop dream of Dr. Martin Luther King?

If only our leaders, black and white, would dig deep in their hearts and reach out to black communities and the inner cities to show that personal responsibility, and not the welfare system, is the way to reach the American dream.

To be perfectly honest, many believe that left-wing liberals, in their effort to appear compassionate toward the working poor who cannot or will not take care of themselves, strive to retain their status for their own political gain. Our black American brothers and sisters deserve more!

Our country disregards the fact that children are having babies, that men are leaving their children, that attempting to educate a youngster whose mother may be uneducated is nearly impossible, and who has never met his or her father, and whose siblings often have many different fathers.

This issue must be faced and solved. If not, the poor will continue to overwhelm the country. It is troublesome that many black individuals are being led to support programs that are destroying them.

A child's social and emotional advancement is strongly affected by his or her home environment. That environment is connected to a child's later capacity to be successful in school and form significant social relationships throughout life. Children from two-parent homes generally tend to have better scholastics and social results. Then again, children who pass up major opportunities for positive early experiences have a higher chance of later problems such as adult criminal behavior and continuing generational poverty.

Picking up a recent edition of the Memphis *Commercial Appeal*, my mind could not help but relate to two front-page articles, as I wondered if I was being negative in connecting the two articles. The first article was "Tenants suffer, say repairs aren't made," which describes the poor condition of the federally subsidized apartment where Teresa Jeans, a single welfare mother, lives with her eight children—the youngest two months old.

Teresa describes her apartment as having a moldy, broken refrigerator. The kitchen counters are falling apart, the window frames regularly falling off, and the stove is unusable because of a leaky gas line. The living room and bedrooms have holes in the walls made by rats, exposing electrical wiring. Windows are broken. The hallway is dark, with no working lights. The bathroom roof is leaking, and the doors are missing knobs.[58]

The second article, entitled "Gunfire abruptly snatches two teens," describes the killing of two innocent teenagers at the hands of other teens. Is there a common denominator between the two articles? Many would answer yes, as statistics show time and again the correlation between children's upbringing in a single parent home and how that environment affects their outcome.[59]

········•••••●•••••·····

In a December 4, 2015, speech, President Barack Obama declared income "inequality" to be "the defining challenge of our time." It is time for me to confess a deep dark secret I have been hiding most of my life: I suffer from income inequality. There are millions of people who make more money than I do, and it has affected my life.

Working in management with the Tennessee Valley Authority for thirty years, my bosses made more than I did. Working at FedEx, I didn't make as much money as Fred Smith.

But thank God for all these people and companies that were responsible for me having a job and affecting my life in a positive way. Was this fair? Absolutely. As long as I had the opportunity through hard work and dedication, it was up to me to make a success of my life.

Many people are of the belief that income "inequality" is a part of the rationality espoused by liberals who need more people addicted to government entitlements and, in turn, gaining their loyalty.

In reality, the top 50 percent of workers in the United States pay 97 percent of the taxes. The top 2 percent earn 19 percent of all wages, yet pay 52 percent of all taxes. Since nearly 50 percent of the populace pays no federal income tax at all, you can see that the wealthier individuals in our society are already supporting the less fortunate to a great extent.[60]

Disparity is genuine, but it's not the result of tax cuts. It's the result of the breakdown of family structure, and unless we find a way to turn around the culture of unwed childbearing and revive marriage, the gap between classes will continue to grow. The success, and possibly the survival, of our nation may well rely on restoring the stability of the traditional family.

Today, we have a tendency to punish the successful and sponsor the unsuccessful. It used to be the other way around, which motivated people to become, if not successful, then at least self-sufficient. Actually, the hard-working affluent business owners are primarily responsible for the jobs that allow us to have a middle class in this country.

The Memphis *Commercial Appeal* recently ran an article entitled "Inequality in Memphis/Disparate Destinies," a story about income in one neighborhood being greater than in another. In response to the story, one responder wrote: "It is indeed sad that fifty years of the Great Society have increased poverty, destroyed families, discouraged true charity, created disincentives to work and made the poor in bondage to government handouts."

Income inequality is not the problem. The real problem is opportunity restriction—restrictions individuals put on themselves, and which government takes advantage of with overregulation.

Why do incomes vary? First there is education—those at the top tend to be more successful and have more. At the bottom are individuals who chose not to make education a priority. In the United States, every child has the chance to get a free education through high school. As a rule, children who leave behind this open door are left to look for rapidly disappearing unskilled jobs.

Today, the philosophy promoted by the income "inequality" crowd is one of victimization. Many of those in the poverty group are erroneously told they are casualties in light of the fact that successful people have stolen from them what is legitimately theirs. I feel sorry for those who believe they are victims and don't do their own research.

The concern should not be the amount of money others make, but rather how much you can make if you put forth a concentrated effort and embrace the qualities that can make one successful. Those who make what I once earned and think they can never earn more are being told a lie. Realizing this is the first step to improving one's income and one's life.

Poor people don't succeed through socialism. They succeed by being free from government reliance, obtaining an education and then a job, working hard, then getting married and having children when they can afford to take care of them.

Unless individuals choose to get the basic free education afforded them, and unless we solve the teen pregnancy problem, this disparity in incomes will always be with us.

There will always be people who ignore the opportunities open to them. They won't realize that the rich got that way through education, hard work, and taking advantage of opportunities to learn new things.

Incomes will never be the same. The government can't impose uniform incomes. Excessively taxing the people who are successful and create jobs for the rest of us won't help the poor. Government can only lay the foundation for equality of opportunity. The door is open and waiting for those of us who are willing to sacrifice and work hard. The opportunity is there for the taking.

Contrary to what some politicians and mainstream media would have you believe, the American dream is open to all Americans. As columnist Cal Thomas stated, "Envy, greed and entitlement are not the things that built America, or sustained her through numerous wars and a Great Depression."

Ladders of opportunity—part of the strength and fabric of this country—are there for the taking, as opposed to being kept in bondage due to government dependency.

*Chapter 6*

# THE TRADITIONAL FAMILY

Families are a collection of personalities and our
search for the perfect family will frustrate us.

What's wrong with our generation? I believe it's a lack
of guidance in the home. We live in a day and age when
God's original plan for the family is virtually nonexistent.
Are we expecting too much from young men and women
who don't have a healthy role model to look up to?

Not too many years ago, marriage played a critical role
in raising children. In most cases, the financial benefits of
marriage are substantial. Marriage among families with
children is an extremely important factor in promoting
economic self-sufficiency.

When compared with children in two-parent homes,
children raised by single parents are more apt to have
emotional and behavioral problems, be victims of abuse,
use illegal drugs, be more aggressive, engage in criminal

behavior, and have poor academic performance, including being expelled from school and dropping out of high school. Many of these negative outcomes are associated with the higher poverty rates of single mothers when compared with children in intact married homes.

Mitch Pearlstein's book *From Family Collapse to America's Decline* gives some of the connections between family breakdown and economic collapse. The statistics are familiar. In 1970, 85.2 percent of children under eighteen lived in a two-parent family. In 2013, it was 68 percent and dropping. Forty percent of births in America are now to unwed parents. Broken down by ethnic group, the figures are 30 percent among whites, 50 percent for Hispanics, and 70 percent for blacks.

It is no secret or accident that the decline of marriage in America largely began with the War on Poverty and the proliferation of welfare programs that resulted. Evidence is clear that most of our social ills can be traced back to the breakdown of morality, the movement away from traditional values with personal responsibility to a system with a lack of morals and personal irresponsibility.

When the War on Poverty began, there was only one welfare program—Aid to Families with Dependent Children (AFDC), to assist single parents. Today, dozens of programs provide a plethora of benefits to single mothers with children, including Temporary Assistance to Needy Families (TANF), the Women, Infants, and Children (WIC) food program, Supplemental Security Income (SSI), food stamps, child nutrition programs, Head Start, school breakfast and lunch programs, summer food programs, Low Income Home Energy Assistance Program (LIHEAP), public housing and Section 8 housing, and Medicaid. The annual bill to taxpayers is over $12 billion.

This doesn't include the Earned Income Tax Credit, the additional costs to schools that come from increased discipline problems, the special educational costs that increase as the result of chaotic family environments, and the added burdens on Medicare and Medicaid that result from more single older Americans.

Also not included, from a local standpoint, are the millions of taxpayer dollars spent treating noninsured patients at the Regional Medical Center in Memphis for injuries sustained as a result of domestic violence, such as beatings, stabbings, and shootings that occur on a daily basis.

The explosive welfare expansion has encouraged single parenthood in two ways. First, our current welfare state promotes single parenthood. It is not easy for single mothers with only a high school education or less to support children without help from another parent. Welfare programs reduce this difficulty by providing extensive financial support to single parents, thereby eliminating the need for marriage. Since the beginning of the War on Poverty, less-educated mothers have increasingly partnered with the welfare state and the taxpayers rather than with the fathers of their children.

As welfare benefits expanded, government aid began to serve as a surrogate for a husband in the home, and low-income marriage began to diminish. As husbands or boyfriends left the family, the need for more welfare to support single mothers increased. The War on Poverty created a destructive cycle: welfare promoted the decline of marriage, which created a need for more welfare.

There have never been more fathers voluntarily abandoning their children in the history of the world. Rather than treating the cause of this tragic situation, we continue to treat the symptom.

A father's absence in the home is traumatic for the rest of the family. Today's society likes to pretend it doesn't matter, that it's okay for the children not to have a dad, but in many cases the consequences can be dire. Unfortunately, the disappearance of fathers is now practically the norm.

Almost one of every four children in the United States resides in a home without the biological dads, both black and white. For black children, it's less than half. Incarceration and drug usage have certainly played a role in this. However, the new social trend says it's okay for a man or a woman to be careless, for him to wander away from his responsibilities because he is young and immature, for her to have a baby on her own because the clock is ticking, and, really, she doesn't need a man for anything more than sperm. Tragically, this is the new morality—the new American mind-set.

Dr. Lasimba Gray Jr. was the editor of an amazing article appearing in the Memphis *Commercial Appeal* recently. Dr. Gray, who is black, is senior pastor of New Sardis Baptist Church and a Faith-in-Memphis panelist. His article is entitled "Churches must take Initiative to fix Problem of Poor Parenting." Dr. Gray's article states:

I recently read with great interest an account of juvenile elephants causing havoc in a sanctuary of rescued elephants. The behavioral scientists were brought in to observe and offer solutions to the problem. These young elephants were attacking other elephants, destroying property, and constantly charging the fence, attempting to break out. After a very short time of observation, one crackerjack expert said, "Here is the problem: All grown male elephants have been removed, and these juveniles have no limits and no authoritative figure to look up to. The problem can be solved by simply returning some bull elephants to this sanctuary." The suggestion was followed and immediately the symptoms of destruction and unruly behavior improved.

Many people say it is okay, that the absence of the father has no impact on the child, that a father is not irreplaceable, and that his disappearance leaves no lasting effect. But statistics on poverty, drug use, education, and incarceration suggest otherwise.

• • • • • • • ● • • • • • • • •

If only lower-income heterosexuals were as eager to marry as some homosexuals, the United States would be a much stronger country. Actually, this sentence might be misleading. From the intense publicity, it may seem that gays are impatient to reach the altar, but it may not be true. Surveys in other countries where same sex marriage is legal have found small numbers of homosexuals seeking marriage (between 2 and 6 percent in Belgium and Holland). Is it possible that legalizing same-sex marriage is sought mostly for symbolic reasons? Imagine if only a fraction of the attention we devote to gay marriage was directed to the state of heterosexual marriage, we might begin to see the true emergency.

Barack Obama spoke about income inequality in an address made during his presidency, but failed to mention one of the biggest contributors to rising inequality in America: the marriage gap.

Sadly, marriage is decaying very fast. As recently as the 1980s, only 13 percent of the children of mothers with at least a high school education were born outside of marriage, according to a report from the National Marriage Project. Today it is 44 percent. Even more serious is the recent trend showing that 53 percent of babies are born to single women under age thirty. Children of this moderately educated class of parents are beginning to experience family breakdown and instability at rates more closely resembling the poor than the upper middle class.

Those who graduate from college are more likely to choose a family life reminiscent, if not quite identical, to the 1950s ideal. High school dropouts are unlikely to marry at all. Their family life in most cases is likely to be chaotic, featuring cohabitation, short marriages, and high rates of instability.

W. Bradford Wilcox of the National Marriage Project reports that "cohabiting couples have a much higher breakup rate than do married couples, a lower level of household income, and a higher level of child abuse and domestic violence." There is no substitute for two married parents who work together to care for their children and contribute to a growing community.

Without the basics of security and stability in their personal lives, many couples not destined for marriage waste good years in impermanent arrangements, often becoming parents. Without the permanence of marriage, people find it much more difficult to rise out of poverty or maintain middle-class lifestyles. They are also far less happy.

Jerome Wright, a local African American journalist who wrote that whites who say they grew up poor but still made a successful life states, "Yes, but I will bet a lot of them grew up in a different era, in a world where family foundations were more stable and opportunity for advancement were more abundant."

Absolutely! In the early 1960s and earlier, two-parent families were the norm for blacks and whites. Is it any coincidence that the breakdown of the traditional American family, particularly in the African American population, began with President Lyndon Johnson's Great Society, which was the beginning of massive government dependency?

Dr. Benjamin Scafidi, professor of economics at Kennesaw State University, explains that "high rates of divorce and failure to marry mean that many more Americans enter late middle age without a spouse to help them manage chronic illnesses or to help care for them if they become disabled. The flight from marriage is transforming the complexion of American society—increasing inequality and decreasing self-sufficiency."

As Kay Hymowitz has written: "Marriage patterns are creating a caste system in a country that had traditionally enjoyed relative equality. Among the well educated, marriage rates have remained very stable over the past several decades. College graduates are mostly rearing their children in orderly, supportive environments in which kids are taught to study hard, delay pregnancy, and plan for the future. But 54 percent of the children of high school dropouts are illegitimate. Their parents' lives are marked by financial stress, conflict and turmoil."

With income and education closely linked, the educated are raising children who have the mind-set to become successful themselves, and the poor are continuing to have children under circumstances that virtually condemn their offspring to poverty.

We have been providing more and more money to schools for decades, and where is the payoff? Government entitlement programs have been around for the last fifty years. Again, where is the payoff? Not only is poverty worse than it was fifty years ago, but the end result is an explosion of crime and violence such as the country has never seen. Reading the same tired solutions and the same excuses for poverty such as more money needed for education, more government programs needed for the poor, and the new excuse—wealth concentrated in the hands of a few—is like hearing a recording over and over.

Jim Clifton, chairman of Gallup, wrote in his book *The Coming Jobs War* of the failure of educational experts and the government to fix the education problem in our country. Clifton states: "There are more than 75 million students enrolled in schools in the United States— successors of today's business leaders. The problem is, approximately 30 percent of those students will drop out or fail to graduate on schedule. About 50 percent of minorities are dropping out. This gives the rest of the developed world a huge advantage over the United States in the upcoming economic wars.

"If this problem isn't fixed fast," says Clifton, "the United States will lose the next worldwide, economic, job-based war because its players can't read, write, or think as well as their competitors." Even more deadly, Gallup suspects that those students' spirits and hope are being irreparably broken.[61]

Educational professionals in the United States will quickly admit that the best science and efforts are nowhere near finding a solution to this problem. The Bill & Melinda Gates Foundation put together the best education scientists in the country, with a cost of over $2 billion, to experiment with several thousand K-12 schools in an attempt to reduce the dropout rate. In 2015, the Memphis city school system received $2 million from this foundation, No success. The government put $4.35 billion into the "Race to the Top" fund, with no improvement yet in learning.

Only 17 percent of charter schools outperform regular public schools. Institutions and universities are trying to solve this problem, or at least see some improvement. So far, all have failed. Sure, there are exceptions of a brilliant few who have performed magic at a school here or there, but the vast majority has not.

Should Americans blame the teachers' unions protecting less qualified teachers, or should they blame it on broken families and bad parenting? Are we treating the symptoms rather than the cause? America bounces around among all these solutions. None seem to work.

Many Americans might believe that government has to spend more money on education. Some leaders also agree that this is the solution. But Gallup continues to find that more money is rarely the solution to big problems. In fact, sometimes the bigger the problem, the less expensive the solution. What's expensive is trying to fix after-the-fact outcomes rather than creating solutions that get to the root cause of the problems. This is leadership at its worst.

Looking at current trends, 43 percent of black males drop out of high school, and of that percentage, more than half eventually go to prison. These statistics help local leaders know how many prisons they need to build, but they don't tell them anything about how to turn at-risk young people around.

What reverses this? Knowing what causes the dropout moments before it happens and the strategies to prevent it. This actually isn't that hard: Gallup has found that kids drop out of school when they lose hope to graduate. It's not always because they are lured into gangs or have to work a low-paying job to help support their family. What can change this sense of hopelessness?

The reason kids lose hope of graduating is because they feel discouraged about what is ahead and start psychologically dropping out. Some kids, both black and white, may be mentally limited. Many students perform poorly in school and feel they are already a failure. Having little vision or excitement for the future can also be the cause of dropping out. Students need to be rescued before they lose hope in the future. And when they aren't caught in time, they don't just drop out of school; they are in danger of dropping out of life.

This can be fixed if America placed more emphasis on the cause versus the effects of hopelessness. Therefore, the emphasis should be built on hope rather than on grades, because loss of hope precedes bad grades, truancy, and dropouts. Gallup scientists have come to the conclusion that hope predicts better academics and better graduation rates than grades or test scores.

Parents and teachers would be smart to consider managing a student's confidence and hope more so than the mechanics of reading, writing, and arithmetic. And the reward for a student may not be just graduating but rather a job—even better, an exciting career path.

Are we overlooking opportunities for young men and women that do not necessarily involve college life? Not all kids are suited for college. Not all kids want to go to college. The school system is designed to encourage and prepare students to attend college and obtain a degree. Much can be said, however, for technical and trade school training. Many good-paying blue-collar jobs are available and obtainable for those with aptitudes in the various trades.

Schools are not equipped to address family problems. That is the responsibility of the parents and the individual. Unfortunately, the government often intervenes and responds by throwing more handouts without anything being required in return and without programs to encourage change or reverse negative behaviors.

· · · · · · · ● · · · · · · · · · ·

The Brookings Institute has recently published a report pointing out the part the traditional family plays in achieving the American dream as compared with the general family breakdown to poverty. According to Brookings, the best defense against poverty is the intact family. But liberal ideas and government dependency weaken the family in two ways:

1. Removing parental responsibility to take care of the family. If the man wants to jump from one woman to another, impregnating some along the way, no worry, the government is there to pick up the tab, absolving him of any responsibility.

2. Absolving women from their responsibilities. If an unmarried woman gets pregnant, Uncle Sam is there to pick up the bills for medical care before and after birth of the child, along with food, diapers, day care, housing, etc.

*Choice* is more than a six-letter word. Welfare programs opened the door for an explosion of out-of-wedlock births. If the right to have children has nothing to do with marriage but everything to do with choice, how does society handle the welfare poor who choose not to marry but have multiple children by different men?

Here again, Johnson's "Great Society" was intended to eliminate child poverty. However, the traditional family breakdown and growth of single-parent families can explain its failure.

Tragically, if you have only one parent around, and/or your mother has ten or more children by age thirty, life is probably going to be chaotic for all of that family. Unfortunately, our system both facilitates and perpetuates such behavior and life choices.

We talk endlessly about this issue—youth violence, domestic violence, and weakening of parental authority, but no one will make the obvious association that the common denominators for these social ills are:

1. Absence of fathers in their children's lives.
2. Government dependency that perpetuates freedom from responsibility.
3. Poor women having out-of-wedlock children they cannot afford.
4. Years of Democratic government has allowed women to be sexually active without accepting responsibility. Some of our leaders may believe they are helping but, in the end, are destroying the family and the hope for these women to escape poverty.

Why do black leaders and ministers neglect to use their influence to encourage moral values? The issue should not be racism, but faith and ethics. Not an attitude of get the most out of government that you can: a variety of women ... a house full of babies.

As George Gilder points out in his book *Men and Marriage*, during the last twenty years, middle-class blacks acquired a net four million skilled jobs, getting new skilled work at a pace between three and five times as fast as whites, while millions of unskilled job openings were shunned by poor blacks. The social relationship no longer revolves around the male as provider and female as procreator. Rather the woman is both provider and procreator.

The welfare system immortalizes this behavior. It is just too easy to produce children outside of marriage when the federal government is so willing to step in and care for them from cradle to grave.

The facts are all too clear. The black family of today lies nearly in ruins, and the white family is rapidly following suit. Tragic, as values are learned through family. With so many children born into families with no father present, core values and family structure are missing from daily life. Deprived of a traditional family life, many of the young people seek pleasure or needs of the moment. As the saying goes, "Sex is for the moment; motherhood is forever."

Family is where we first learn and pass down a foundation of values and rules. Without this structure, families can become a breeding ground for hopelessness. Moms and dads, both black and white, should be responsible for teaching their children values and how to develop a work ethic that defeats poverty. Children learn how to treat others by observing how their moms and dads treat each other.

A friend, whose child I will call Rachel, attended White Station High School in Memphis, where blinds were falling off windows, ceiling tiles were missing, and whose leaky roof promised wet floors on rainy days, espoused the excellent education her daughter received there. Despite the school's physical condition, White Station ranks as one of the top schools in the state for producing merit scholars.

What separated Rachel's experience from that of other students who did not learn while there? Or the thousands of students who attend newer multimillion dollar schools in the city? Was it quality of home life—the ability and willingness of both parents to say no and back it up; and the unspoken expectation that you are going to get an education, get a job, be a law-abiding citizen, and have a family at some point when you can afford to do so?

US citizens, both black and white, are forced to pay taxes to support countless illegitimate children rather than address the root cause of the problem. Rap music containing vulgar and racist words resonate through the halls and streets of black neighborhoods. Crime and illegitimacy rates make it all too clear that our young people are getting the message.

According to the US Census Bureau, in areas where family life is strong, 70 percent of blacks live above the poverty line, 60 percent own stocks, and 49 percent live in middle-class neighborhoods. Black life in America is successful where family lifestyles and values are strong.

The single biggest issue facing the majority of African Americans today is struggling to raise numerous children in single-parent homes.

So why, then, do our politicians fight for the plethora of social programs that have contributed to the major African American problem today?

Trying to raise children outside marriage is a constant struggle. Figures from the Department of Human Services show that single black mothers head 48 percent of all black households today. According to the Population Resource Bureau, about 80 percent of all children referred to psychiatric hospitals are from single-parent homes. Yet liberals are at a loss to understand why, after fifty years of liberal policies that have contributed to this major problem in the United States, our poverty rate has not improved.

Most liberals and black leaders tend to ignore the fact that our federal government makes illegitimacy a popular trend by providing medical care, child care, food and shelter, and various other benefits for teenage girls who have children before marriage. Too many of our young women are making welfare a career choice as opposed to temporary assistance.

Birth rates to unmarried teenagers have doubled since the 1960s. According to CURE, teenage girls accounted for 30 percent of all unwed births in 1996. Half of these young mothers were on welfare within one year of having their first child, and 77 percent were on welfare within five years. The homicide rate for young African American males in the United States is ten times that of whites. Despite these statistics, black leaders cry out over perceived racism as opposed to working to solve the problems resulting from children being raised in fatherless homes and the perpetual cycle of crime and poverty created by the federal government's manipulation of their lives.

Students in poor areas in Tennessee see significant gains in prekindergarten classrooms, but quickly lose that growth over the next few years, a Vanderbilt University study shows. The study, a partnership between Vanderbilt and the Tennessee Department of Education, took five years and cost $6 million. The Tennessee pre-K program known as TN-VPK spends $85 million statewide annually on preschool for at-risk students.

The study found that children in the state pre-K programs "made greater gains in achievement than children who did not attend pre-K, and were considered by their teachers as better prepared for kindergarten. By the end of kindergarten, however, the children who did not attend VPK had caught up and were equally competitive with those who attended VPK," the study found. And by second grade, both groups of kindergarten students were still lagging behind national averages.

Prekindergarten development should occur primarily within the home and is the responsibility of parents. Supplementing this education, to some degree, can be done by churches and volunteer groups. The education problem is a symptom of a cultural sickness. We have spent trillions of dollars unsuccessfully treating this symptom.

Schools are being encouraged to provide federally funded preschool services: health clinics, social services, parent education, welfare assistance, family counseling, and other services under the Elementary and Secondary Education Act. Goals 2000 was started to help children select career paths.

Former President George W. Bush created the No Child Left Behind program because of his concern over poor test scores primarily in our large inner cities such as Detroit; Washington, DC; Los Angeles; and Atlanta. Many of these students are exposed to violence in the home and fight to stay alive walking to and from school. These are the children most likely to be left behind. Despite what politician's advocate, being left behind cannot be resolved by our government. The solution to this sad circumstance can only be found in a return to strong families versus a culture of generational single households where the federal government has taken on the role of being a father figure and provider for our children.

Giving the government more power to assume responsibility of the family has been tragic for inner-city schools and neighborhoods. Perpetuating a cycle of poverty doesn't solve anything. The federal government's solution for solving every crisis is allocating ever-increasing sums of taxpayer money.

A traditional family structure offers the best way to learn and pass down values and morals. It provides the framework for which to carry out life's meaning, the educational process, and, in turn, to develop a work ethic that defeats poverty. Without structure, the family is in danger of becoming a breeding ground for hopelessness.

# Chapter 7

# POVERTY INC.

Prosperity does not come from government and politics, but from freedom and personal responsibility.

Thousands of people have left Memphis since the 2008 economic downturn, but the city is not only surviving, but benefiting from the $5 billion pumped into the local economy by the poverty industry.

Memphis, home to half of the region's two hundred thousand low-income households, ranks regularly among the country's poorest metropolitan areas. But less understood is a thriving industry that has quietly grown up around the city's poor: Poverty Inc.

The business of poverty now generates over $5 billion a year in the city. That's the surprising and probably underestimated figure reported in the Memphis *Commercial Appeal*. During 2012 and early 2013, the newspaper compiled an analysis of the impact of Poverty Inc. on the city of Memphis.

According to the newspaper's report, poverty is a huge part of the Memphis economy. The direct payments to poor people living in Memphis, along with the money generated and spent by hundreds of nonprofit organizations, government antipoverty programs, and poverty-related businesses easily top $5 billion a year now.[62]

This number doesn't include anything related to churches or charities such as United Way that also work with the poor. Memphis has a reputation for giving, both in charitable contributions and in tithing to churches. In fact, the *Chronicle of Philanthropy* ranks Memphis as the second-most generous city among the fifty largest cities in America. The *Commercial Appeal* estimates there are over 180 philanthropic organizations in Memphis working with the poor to alleviate poverty.

The newspaper's report clearly shows that poverty has been a booming industry for Memphis over the last thirty years. Poverty Inc. has grown enormously while blue-collar manufacturing jobs here have declined.

Beginning around 1980, government funds coming into Memphis to fight poverty totaled about $155 million. In 2015, those direct payments to fight poverty were over $5 billion.

After fifty years of additional spending in Memphis to fight poverty, the 2012 US Census still showed Memphis to be among the three poorest large cities in America. These same statistics for 2012 also show that poor, unmarried African American women now have the largest percentage of babies in Memphis.[63]

Neither the poverty rate nor the number of poor people in Memphis seems to have declined—despite the billions of dollars of federal, state, and local dollars that have become an integral part of the Memphis economy. And therein is the dilemma. Poverty Inc. is a huge business and a thriving business, with the intended goal of reducing poverty in this city. But is it actually working to reduce poverty here? Or has Poverty Inc. taken on something of a life of its own in Memphis, diverting resources away from other economic growth opportunities? Is Poverty Inc. becoming a corporation that simply builds upon our city's culture of poverty?

Poverty Incorporated—the human costs of poverty in Memphis—now strains the public school system, the criminal justice system, and the vast philanthropic services network that today is supporting tens of thousands of Memphis families and over half of all African American children living in the city.

Memphis and poverty are united in deep and lasting ways. To truly challenge that bond, difficult discussions are needed to determine if Poverty Inc. is in this city's best interest, or ultimately will be its undoing.

The amount of money pumped into Memphis's poverty industry is five times FedEx's annual local payroll, according to a study by the *Commercial Appeal* and the University of Memphis. FedEx, for example, is Memphis's largest company. Yet, these federal outlays dwarf the world's largest global transportation industry's $1 billion-plus annual Memphis payroll.

"There's a tremendous log of economic activity that revolves around the billions of dollars of commerce associated with poor people," said University of Memphis economist John Gnuschke, who participated in the newspaper's study.

Despite Memphis having the highest poverty rate of any metropolitan area with more than one million residents, the poor are still able to sustain hundreds of shops, stores, and offices. This is due primarily to the social safety net, otherwise known as Poverty Inc.

Just over $3 billion flowed from Washington for the one hundred thousand least well-off households in Memphis in 2010. In 2015, that amount nearly doubled. However, this tidal wave of cash has never affected the poverty rate.

Although wages for thousands of Memphis families fall below the poverty line, they are still consumers. These one hundred thousand individuals eke out just enough aid individually to get by. Collectively, these one hundred thousand households support a wide slice of the Memphis economy.

At a time when policy makers in Washington are talking about cutting back federal spending, the *Commercial Appeal* set out to figure what share of the poverty business ties directly to federal government aid. The review shows Washington accounts for more than 60 percent of the $5.39 billion, which excludes all federal grants, such as law enforcement funds, and the $300 million going to Memphis City Schools. The study included only cash outlays that go directly to poor citizens.

Businesses from pawn shops to health clinics, whose clients are largely poor, account for over $850 million. Baptist Memorial Hospital, for example, provided over $55 million worth of uncompensated care in its 2015 budget year.[64]

Besides impoverished families, one of every three working Memphians earn just enough to get tax credits meant to lift them out of poverty. In 2012, nearly 103,000 city residents received over $3 million in tax refunds related directly to these earned income tax credits.[65]

Just how big is the poverty trade in Memphis compared to other sectors of the economy? Tax refunds, for example, get spent at pawn shops. Food stamps are used at dollar stores. What's clear is that Washington stands out as an economic driver.

While an enormous flow of cash fuels the poverty trade in Memphis, the money barely touches the tip of the iceberg. Unfortunately, the flow has risen, and the poverty rate remains high. Medicaid disbursements, for example, rose 62 percent between 2000 and 2010. Food stamps, now called the Supplemental Nutrition Assistance Program (SNAP), quadrupled as the jobless rate climbed from 3.6 percent to 11.1 percent.[66]

In some neighborhoods, nearly 20 percent of households report an annual income of less than $10,000—enough to sustain some businesses. "Our customers are really good people. They just don't have bank accounts. We're their bank," said Ann Agee-Gates, managing partner of Happy Hocker, a pawnshop on East Parkway in Memphis.

Sustained by safety net programs, an unemployed single resident of South Memphis described how she survives. Add up the food stamps and her parent's rent subsidy and Social Security, and they live as if they earned $400 per week.

"I've put my life on hold. I've learned to live basically," said the woman, who declined to be identified. She said she left the workforce to take care of an elderly parent.

The parent has since recovered, and the woman could now return to work, but she said she is just comfortable enough to stay home. She lives in her parent's apartment; Medicaid and Social Security checks cover the basics. Energy is used sparingly to keep the monthly bill under $150. Rent costs the two of them less than $150 per month after the Section 8 subsidy payment. Her Earned Income Tax Credit exceeded $1,000 last year. She contributes her $200 per month worth of food stamps. "Food stamps make me able to live at a standstill." she said. "It plagues me that I'm not working, but right now I don't have to."[67]

Multiplying this scenario by hundreds of thousands in the Memphis area alone, and as Star Parker relates: "Uncle Sam's Plantation is alive and well."

A recent article in the *Washington Post* entitled "Government Aid Props up Factory Wages for Many," reveals a massive amount of government programs designed to help single-parent families who have lower paying jobs.

Take the case of Philadonna Wade. Philadonna has a job that Americans often associate with the American dream. She works at a Ford chassis plant in Ohio where truck axles are finished before they ship to the big Ford factories nearby.[68]

Manufacturing jobs once offered good wages, but Philadonna is a temporary worker, employed through a staffing agency making $9.50 an hour. As a single mother, she doesn't make nearly enough money to take care of her four children. Taxpayers help her make up the difference. "I get energy assistance; I get food stamps; I get Medicaid," she said. "Every bit of public assistance there is, I get it."

Wade's experience is not unusual, researchers at the University of California-Berkeley have described in a new report. The report says one-third of families of "frontline manufacturing production workers," are enrolled in government benefit programs, costing state and local governments about $10 billion a year on average since 2009. These workers, roughly six million, represent about half of all manufacturing workers. They include metal workers, assemblers, and machinists, but not management or software employees.

Many of the workers who draw government benefits work full time in jobs that, like Wade's, are staffed through temp agencies. Nearly half of the families of production workers who were employed through staffing agencies received government welfare of some kind, the report found.

Wade says her job is an improvement from her previous employment at the Family Dollar store, but the added pay has reduced her government food stamp payments. A single mother, she lives with her four children in public housing. She would like to earn more money, she said, and she would also like people to stop stigmatizing folks who accept government help to get through.

## Chapter 8

# HOPE FOR THE FUTURE

Everybody can be great because anybody can
serve. You don't have to have a college degree to
serve. You don't have to make your subject and
your verb agree to serve. You don't have to know
the second theory of thermodynamics in physics
to serve. You only need a heart full of grace.
A soul generated by love.
—Dr. Martin Luther King Jr.

Dr. Roland Fryer, the youngest African American to
receive tenure at Harvard University and the first to win
a John Bates Clark Medal, said he decided to do a study
of what is going on when it comes to racial differences
in police use of force. He and his student researchers
spent about three thousand hours assembling detailed
data from police reports in ten of our larger inner cities.
They examined 1,332 shootings between 2000 and 2015
with the goal of determining if police officers were quicker
to fire at black suspects.[69]

Calling it "the most surprising result of my career," Dr. Fryer states that when it came to the most lethal form of force—police shootings—the study finds no racial bias; in fact, statistics clearly showed whites were much more likely to be shot in police confrontations than blacks. The study also showed that black men and women were more likely to be stopped and frisked than whites.

In response to Black Lives Matter, the *Washington Post* launched a case-by-case study of police shootings. After a year of research, the following was found: Police use force mainly to protect human life; the use of force against unarmed suspects is rare, and the use of force against black Americans is largely proportional to their share of the violent crime rate. The *Post* also reports: Although black men make up only 6 percent of the US population, they account for 50 percent of the homicides in the United States.

The data clearly indicate that police, rather than showing bias against black men, have showed considerable restraint in dealing with them. In fact, a new study shows police are 20 percent less likely to shoot black suspects.

So why then does the African American population feel so strongly that they are victims of racially motivated mistreatment and brutality by the police? The simple answer is our liberal news media. When have you seen national coverage of a white person shot by police? We know it happens—the statistics are clear. The news media is in the business of reporting news—the bigger and more explosive the story the better. The story of a white person brutalized or shot by police does not make headlines and is seldom reported.

Is the problem really police discrimination? Or is the real problem that more black youths are raised by and get their values from the streets, rather than from a stable family with responsible parents? Why not learn to respect authority, whether it is a parent, teacher, or law enforcement?

We have had a breakdown in American culture. In the world I knew growing up, we were taught by our parents and teachers to respect authority figures: police, teachers, government, and country.

At one time, children of all races were taught to respect authority; and more so, to respect the rights of other people. Children were taught to keep their hands to themselves and not to take things that didn't belong to them. If you were confronted by a neighbor, a teacher, or even a policeman, you did what they said to do without fail. There would always be time later to redress your situation in court or in some other way.

Over the course of a year, I've watched many videos of adults and children placing law enforcement officers across the country in situations where they must use their police powers to enforce the law. The latest video shows a police officer arresting a sixteen-year-old female student who refused to comply with a lawful order, and who physically assaulted the officer after repeated attempts by both school officials and the officer for voluntary compliance.

In many instances, these are young people that need our cultivation, guidance, and teaching. Otherwise, it may be too late when you hear of them sitting in the back of a squad car at the tender age of sixteen or older, crying out for their momma! None of us want to hear or see that and realize it's too late for them and us.

Crime is not a problem of law enforcement. It is a community problem that in part needs to be solved by parents and the people in our communities. Cultural issues and bad policy are not the fault of the police.

Rather than bashing law enforcement, citizens should encourage police officers to do their jobs. Today we have a cultural dysfunction in our cities where too many lawyers are investigating too many cops. As with any other occupation, there are good and bad, but the overwhelming majority of policemen have the best interest of the public at heart. You never know when a policeman or law enforcement officer will save your life or the life of a loved one

• • • • • • • • •●●• • • • • • • • •

The kind of love we all need to share correctly describes a recent incident that occurred in a Memphis park. A white police officer was parked in his squad car when an African American lady with two small children saw him and decided to stop. As the woman approached the police officer, she simply stated she wanted to pray for him, specifically for his safety.

After the prayer, the officer said he expressed his gratitude as best he could, but she really had no idea how much that had meant to him. Her little boy handed the officer a wilted flower that looked as if it had been in his pocket for a week. At that moment, he said it was the most beautiful flower he'd even seen.

The police officer said his prayer is that by sharing this encounter, it may encourage others to give people a chance, regardless of race or profession. "You simply cannot judge an entire group of people because of the actions of some. Don't hate evil more than you love good," said the policeman.

Another encouraging sign for our city was the recent marches and prayer vigils held in several Memphis African American communities. These were peaceful protests against black-on-black crimes: murder, robberies, gangs, drugs, domestic abuse, and rape.

The Memphis Urban League has initiated a new program called "Save our Sons," which is aimed at helping young black men find gainful employment. The program will include free job and educational training for unemployed and underemployed men in Memphis and Shelby County between the ages of eighteen and thirty-five, targeting black men in particular. Giving programs such as the "Save our Sons" initiative the support they need will go a long way toward reassuring those who are living in poverty that their community cares about their struggles.

The BRIDGES Organization, in conjunction with the Shelby County Sheriff's Department, is working to organize jailhouse workshops, asking juvenile detainees what youth violence looks like. In a recent workshop, the answers from the detainees who are in jail awaiting trial on charges that include drug possession, firearm possession, assault, rape, and murder, came quickly and easily: fighting, drugs, gangs, shooting, robbing, rape, and abuse.

The detainees were then asked who is to blame for youth violence. Again, the answers came quickly: parents, other African American men, gang members, drug dealers, teachers, and police officers. Then the key question was asked by experts on youth violence. "If we got rid of all these people, would that solve the problem?" The answer was evident to everyone in the room: "of course not."

Here again, we are so politically correct in our society that we are afraid to say the truth. Why not ask these young offenders about the real problem—let them talk to you about their childhoods. Ask them about Mama and Daddy, their family members. Look inside their homes. You may get some revealing answers.

Starting with the school system, our overreaching government, in its quest for sameness, has taken away much of the discipline, respect for authority, respect for each other, respect for property, love of country, and positive desire to succeed. The absence of character-building traits has been successfully explained as a duty of the home, not public education.

While in agreement with this principle, I feel what we are failing to take into consideration is the large percentage of young, single-parent homes where the parents themselves are victims of this void. Sadly, this void is being filled with resulting youth violence.

• • • • • • ●● ● ●● • • • • • • • •

A thought-provoking article written by African American Latrice Ingram appeared in the *Washington Post*. Latrice is a homeschooling mother of four. She writes and speaks mainly on faith, family, and education. Says Latrice:

Tell me you don't understand what it's like to be black. Tell me you don't understand what it's like to fear the things I fear. Tell me you don't have all the answers but you want to know more, you want to help, you want to see change. Don't argue with me about why I'm hurting. Don't argue with me about why I'm angry. Don't try to be right. And please don't try to make me responsible for why all these things are happening. And, after all that, maybe ask to meet me for coffee and listen to my stories and my family's stories. And maybe try to hear me. Try to hear us."

What a wonderful world this could be if we would all make an effort to do as Latrice suggested. I would like to take you up on that cup of coffee, Latrice!

• • • • • • ●● ● ●● • • • • • • • •

On a recent visit to the Vietnam Veterans Memorial Wall in Washington, DC, a range of emotions was evident as families and friends of the deceased heroes paid homage to their loved ones. Visitors with tear-filled eyes passed hands over some of the fifty-eight thousand names engraved in the black granite.

Near the end of the wall, I passed a sobbing African American woman standing alone and rubbing her hand over a name on the warm marble. Her tears tugged at my heart as I stopped, turned around, and walked back to where she was standing. Enveloping her heaving shoulders in my arms, she managed through her sobs to thank me and pointed to a name on the wall. "My Daddy," she said. "It mattered not the color of our skin, nor the skin color of any of the military heroes on the wall, but rather the conditions of our hearts and minds—we were one."

· · · · · ●●●● ● ●●●●·· · · · ·

None of us are able to totally control the negative actions of others, but if we make an effort to respond with kindness and understanding, we'll get through with hope for tomorrow. If we teach our children to see the world this way, I have to believe our lives and the lives of others will change for the better. And if I'm wrong, at least when life sucks us under, and, again to quote Sheryl Sandberg, "You can kick against the bottom, break the surface, and breathe again."

Parenting a child takes complete dedication and years of hard work preparing a foundation for building a successful career or other endeavor. You pour your heart and soul, along with countless hours, into nurturing, developing, and growing a child into something special. Along the way, you experience highs, embarrassing lows, and lessons learned that build strength, character, and leadership—with patience being the key ingredient.

My hope is that parents instill in their children the knowledge and understanding to do what is right—to obey the law and to respect authority. We can all do more by simply listening, caring, and giving attention.

For those kids who don't look to the future with any hope, let's give them that hope. Give them that encouragement so they can become productive members of society!

· · · · · ● ● ● ● ● ● ● ● · · · · · · · · ·

While much of the news in Memphis is disheartening, I cannot let the uplifting story of African American Mose Frazier go unnoticed. Mose, who played football for the University of Memphis, is a gifted athlete with NFL aspirations.

After an upset win over the University of Mississippi football team the previous day, Mose was at his job at Audubon Golf Course early the following morning. As he greeted golfers when they showed up for their regular rounds, he told them, "Just a regular day. I couldn't take off to celebrate or anything. This is my job." Mose spends four mornings a week working at the golf course. To quote Mose, "I love it," he said. "I just like working, period. It just makes me feel better as a man." Asked about his pay, he said, "It's good. I make $12 an hour. It makes me feel independent, like I'm handling my responsibilities."

That's the best part of the story: the feeling of accomplishment that comes with an earned dollar. "It's just something inside of me," said Frazier. "Growing up in a struggle, just seeing the things around me, it motivates me to make a better life."

And in case you're wondering, Mose does not play golf, and he gives a reason for that. "They say it's addictive," he said. "Right now, where I am, I can't let anything distract me from becoming a success."

Beautiful!

· · · · · · ●● ●● · · · · · · · · · ·

Another inspiring story is that of La'Andre Thomas. La'Andre has received a full scholarship to play football for the University of Memphis beginning September 2017. La'Andre's tumultuous life story parallels some of the events described in *The Common Denominator*.

Sitting in his high school football coach's office in Wingfield High a few days after leading his team to a 2-0 start for the first time in nine years, quarterback La'Andre Thomas shook his head at his coach's question. "No," he said. "I don't want to share that." "Thomas is reluctant to share parts of his past," said his older brother Akeem. "He doesn't want anyone to feel sorry for him."

Before he scored six touchdowns in a win against a neighboring school, before he was recruited by the University of Memphis and Southern Mississippi, and before he learned to play football, La'Andre was eating out of dumpsters. When he was five, Thomas lived with his grandmother—"or at least I think she was my grandmother because my mom was adopted," he said—in what he remembers as a shotgun house in an alley off East Fortification Street in Jackson, Mississippi.

La'Andre, who is eighteen, has seven siblings that he knows of. All eight share the same mother, whom La'Andre describes as a drug addict, and all have different fathers. La'Andre says he occasionally communicates with his mother on facebook but has never had a relationship with her. He said he has never met his father.

While living with whom he assumes were his grandparents, La'Andre helped push grocery carts full of belongings, collected cans for money, and dug in dumpsters searching for scraps of food. "That's how we ate," said Thomas. "It was that bad and it got even worse," he said.

Seemingly hesitate, La'Andre said. "I can tell you this much. Between fourth grade and seventh grade, I really didn't have a home."

Around the time he was in fourth grade, he said he moved from the alley into a two-bedroom, one bathroom apartment in Jackson with a woman he refers to as his "auntie" and at least nine others, including his brother Akeem. Only La'Andre's "uncle" worked, and Akeem chipped in by sweeping the floor of a barber shop for five dollars a night. It was here that La'Andre lived without basic necessities. He would sleep with two other kids in a twin-sized bed soaked in urine, Akeem said. They lived without electricity in a home for two years, filling jugs of water with a neighbor's hose after hopping over a fence in the middle of the night. "That's how we took baths, washed our clothes and got water to drink," said Akeem. "One time, we went more than a month without brushing our teeth or taking a bath."

"The worst feeling I think I ever had was just being hungry," La'Andre said, "and knowing you can't do anything about it." He said he once went two days without eating before breaking open a box of instant mashed potatoes.

La'Andre spent as little time at his aunt's house as possible. He often stayed at friend's homes for months at a time. "I wasn't even telling my auntie where I was and nobody asked," he said. "It felt like I was homeless. I was at a time in my life where I felt like no one even cared about me. When you talk about the lowest of the lows, I hope that was it," said La'Andre.

The Memphis community is both excited and humbled to have La'Andre join the Memphis Tiger family. Not only are we thrilled to have someone of his physical ability, but as one who has overcome tremendous odds, La'Andre appears to have what it takes to be a success regardless of the obstacles.

"I don't want to be another statistic," La'Andre said. "I want to start a new foundation. I don't want my family to ever go through what I went through. I want to start a whole new generation. My purpose is bigger than me because one decision can mess up the whole generation behind me. I don't want that. I want to be known as not just a great athlete, but a great human being."

The lesson here: La'Andre Thomas, an amazing role model for today's youth, refused to let his past beat him.

· · · · · · · ● · ● · · · · · · · · ·

When speaking to civic organizations and churches, I am often asked what advice I would give young people today, especially those who are struggling. I tell them that change is possible through hard work, delayed gratification, and never giving up, and that sometimes adversity can become an opportunity. I like to show them by example that hardship can be an advantage if one does not let themselves become a victim. By encouraging people to train their hearts and minds to see the good in everything and everybody, I believe lives will be impacted for the better.

My life has been an open book with seventy-six chapters, and I remember all of them well. Some of them have been happy, some hard, some filled with a little sin, and other chapters sad. I know how this book of my life started, but only God knows when and how He will finish its final chapters.

Our lives are story books that we write for ourselves, wonderfully illustrated by the people we meet. To quote one of my heroes, Dr. Ben Carson: "While much of America seems to be getting more and more divisive, I'm going to be holding doors for strangers, letting people cut in front of me in traffic, greeting all I meet, exercising patience with others and smiling at strangers. I'll do this as often as I have the opportunity. I will not stand idly by and let children live in a world where unconditional love is invisible and being rude is acceptable. Find your way to swing the pendulum in the direction of love—because today, sadly, hate is gaining ground. Love must begin somewhere and love will overcome hate."

Imagine the difference if we each purposefully love a little more.

Always remember that life is precious. When we work hard at it, we are able to make it good for ourselves and for others. Let us all respect each other and come together as a nation. When we do this, the greatest generation can rest knowing there is hope for a new generation.

Joseph Epstein once said, "We do not choose to be born. We do not choose our parents, or the country of our birth. We do not, most of us, choose to die; nor do we choose the time and conditions of our death. But within this realm of choicelessness, we do choose how we live."

# $\mathcal{R}$eferences

## (Endnotes)

1 Tom Terrific, "The Dotson Massacre," Memphis *Commercial Appeal*, http://www.memphiscommercialappeal,com/2008/memphistn

2 Ibid

3 Mark Berman, "Surge in Slayings," *Washington Post*, Jody Callahan, Memphis *Commercial Appeal*.

4 WMC Action News, "New billboard in Orange Mound puts twist on Black Lives Matter," http://wmcactionnews5.com.

5 Tracey Rogers, A Better Mid-South: "Kin Killin' Kin," http://www.wmcactionnews5

6 WREG TV, "Young Men say Kroger mob attack was 'just what kids do,'" http://wregtv.com.

7 Mark Berman, "Surge in Slayings," *Washington Post*, berman@washingtonpost.com.

8 Beth Warren, "Teen dodges adult court after shooting," Memphis *Commercial Appeal*, Warren@commercialappeal.com

9 Beth Warren, "The Tragic Case of Cartrail Robertson," Memphis *Commercial Appeal*, Warren@commercialappeal.com.

10 Ibid.

11 Jerry Askin, "3 Siblings murdered; fourth in jail on murder charge," wmcActionNews5, wmcnews.com.

12 Cassie Owens, "How City Leaders Aim to Break the Poverty Cycle in South Memphis," cdo2106@columbia.edu.

13   Ibid.

14   Ibid.

15   Chris Peck, "Innocents at Risk," Memphis *Commercial Appeal*, http://www.peck@commercialappeal.com

16   Kayleigh Skinner, "Program heals more than bullet wounds, "Memphis *Commercial Appeal*, http://skinner@commercial Appeal.com

17   Ibid

18   John Scalea, University of Maryland Shock Trauma Center, http://scalea@universityofmaryland, edu.

19   Azadeh Ansari, "Chicago's 72 homicides in 2016 is highest in 19 years," *CNN Reports*.

20   Ibid.

21   Ibid

22   David H.Ciscel, University of Memphis, "The Economic Impact of Teen Pregnancy in Memphis/Shelby County, TN," ciscel@bellsouth.net

23   Ibid

24   Ibid

25   Ibid

26   Beth Warren, "Report Paints Bleak Picture," Memphis *Commercial Appeal*, warren@commercialappeal.com.

27   Ibid.

28   Chris Peck, "Innocents at Risk," Memphis *Commercial Appeal*, http://peck@commercialappeal.com

29   Ibid.

30   Ibid.

31   Ibid.

32   Beth Warren, "Report Paints Bleak Picture," Memphis *Commercial Appeal*, http://warren@commercialappeal.com.

33   Chris Peck, "A Step Ahead on Teen Pregnancy," Memphis *Commercial Appeal*, http://peck@commercialappeal.com.

34   Otis Sanford, Suzanne Kerr, Michael Kelley, Jerome Wright, Editorial Board, Memphis *Commercial Appeal*, http:// commercialappeal.com

35   Ibid.

36   Ibid.

37   Jerome Wright, "No Easy Answer for City's Poor," Memphis *Commercial Appeal*, http://wright@commercialappeal.com

38   Ibid.

39   Ibid.

40   Ibid

41   David Waters, Leaders Urge Adults to Guide our Youth," Memphis Commercial Appeal, http://waters@commercialappeal.com

42   Lawrence Buser, "Mom of Slain Toddler Testifies," *Memphis CommercialAppeal*, http://buser@commercialappeal,com.

43   Bill O'Reilly, *Fox News*, "Black leadership not solving problems facing African Americans," http://insider.foxnews.com.

44   Tony Pugh, "Black families fail to make progress," McClatchy Newspapers, http://pugh@mcclatchynewspapers.com.

45   Ibid.

46   Ibid.

47   Ibid.

48   MSNBC staff, "Father of 30, by 11 women, wants support help from the state," http://usnews.msnbc.msn.com

49   Tony Pugh, "Black Families Fail to Make Progress," "New Study re-examines Controversial Report." The *Memphis Commercial Appeal,* http://pugh@mcclatchynewspapers.com

50   Ibid.

51   Ibid.

52   Ibid.

53   Ibid.

54   Ibid.

55   Ibid

56   Ibid

57   Ibid

58   Maria Ines Zamudio, "Tenants suffer, say repairs aren't made," Memphis *Commercial Appeal*, http://zamudio@commercialappeal.com

59   Katie Fretland, "Gunfire abruptly snatches two girls," Memphis *Commercial Appeal*, http://fretland@commercialappeal.com.

60    Kyle Pomerleau, "Summary of Latest Federal Income Tax Data," Center for Federal Tax Policy.

61    Jim Clifton, K-12 Schools—Where Entrepreneurs are Created, *The Coming Jobs War,* Gallup Press, 2011

62    Ted Evanoff, "Poverty Inc.," Memphis *Commercial Appeal,* http://evanoff@commercialappeal.com

63    Ibid.

64    Ibid.

65    Ibid.

66    Ibid.

67    Ibid.

68    Jim Tankersley, "Report: Government aid props up factory wages for many," *Washington Post,* http://tankersley@washingtonpost.com

69    Roland G. Fryer Jr., "An Empirical Analysis of Racial Differences in Police Use of Force," NBER Working Paper No. 22399